RENSSELAER W. LEE was Chairman of the Department of Art and Archaeology at Princeton University from 1955 until his retirement in 1966. He received his Ph.D. degree from Princeton in 1926, and has also taught at Northwestern, Smith, Columbia, and the New York University Institute of Fine Arts. Professor Lee has been Editor-in-Chief of the *Art Bulletin* (1942–44), President of the College Art Association of America (1945–46), and Director of the Committee on Protection of Cultural Treasures in War Areas (1953–61). He is presently a Trustee of the American Academy in Rome, a Councillor of the Mediaeval Academy of America, and President of the Union Académique Internationale.

UT PICTURA POESIS

The Humanistic Theory of Painting

UT PICTURA POESIS

The Humanistic Theory of Painting

by
Rensselaer W. Lee

The Norton Library
W · W · NORTON & COMPANY · INC ·
NEW YORK

Library of Congress Catalog Card No. 67–15820

Published simultaneously in Canada by
George J. McLeod Limited, Toronto

ISBN   0   393   00399   X

PRINTED IN THE UNITED STATES OF AMERICA

4 5 6 7 8 9 0

CONTENTS

PREFACE TO THE 1967 EDITION

THIS ESSAY attempts to define the humanistic theory of painting and to record in broad terms its development from its beginning in the fifteenth century to the eighteenth when new forces in critical thought and in art began to cause its decline. Everywhere in the theory is the fundamental assumption—an assumption which is made no longer—that good painting, like good poetry, is the ideal imitation of human action. From this it follows that painters, like poets, must express general, not local, truth through subjects which education in the Biblical narratives and the Greco-Roman classics has made universally known and interesting; must deploy a rich variety of human emotion; and must aim not merely to please, but also to instruct mankind. This theory, like much of the art of the period, had its roots in antiquity. It was specifically certain famous comparisons of poetry and painting in Aristotle and Horace that prompted the critics of painting, who found no real theory of painting in antiquity, to take over the ancient literary theory pretty much lock, stock, and barrel and make it apply to an art for which it was not originally intended. The results of this process and the changing fortunes of the doctrine through the Renaissance, Mannerist, and Baroque periods are an interesting commentary on the progress of the arts. And if the critics sometimes went astray in forcing a literary aesthetic on the pictorial art, they were, on the whole, more right than wrong. In fact, they found their *raison d'être* for a humanistic theory of painting not only in the prescriptions of ancient authors for a humanistic literature, but in Italian art itself which, from Cimabue and Giotto to Raphael, Michelangelo, and Titian, had been concerned at its best with truth, which is in the highest sense representative of human action and emotion. And, in any case, a direct or implied comparison of painting with poetry was natural enough when the painters, like their ancient forebears, drew so largely for their inspiration on the great poetry of the past and present.

Written some twenty-five years ago, this study, in a sense interdisciplinary, seems to have served the purposes both of art and literary historians, and even, at times, of musicologists. It has been, I am told, useful not only to mature scholars, but to graduate students and undergraduates as well. I hope, then, that its release in book form from its rather stately and inaccessible prison in the *Art Bulletin* will bring some satisfaction both to the teachers who have been good enough to assign it to their students and to the students who have often found it hard to lay their hands on. The opportunity has been taken to make certain corrections in the text, to improve some illustrations where better copy has come to hand, and to add an index.

If I were writing the essay today, its essential argument and conclusions would stand very much as they are. However, I would mitigate the overemphasis of certain judgments. I would not, for instance, condemn out of hand Charles Le Brun's allegorical histories with a clever phrase borrowed from Tennyson, nor would I call Annibale Carracci's *Rinaldo and Armida* in Naples, though it is no masterpiece, an intolerable picture. More important, since the appearance of the essay in 1940, several scholars have published works that valuably supplement or correct what I have written. First among these is Denis Mahon's *Studies in Seicento Art and Theory* (London, 1947), with its important discovery of a fragment of an early seventeenth-century treatise on painting by Giovanni Battista Agucchi that anticipates the theory of Bellori by half a century. In an article entitled "Antique Frameworks for Renaissance Art Theory: Alberti and Pino," in *Marsyas*, Vol. III (1946), Creighton Gilbert demonstrated that it was the Venetian painter and writer Paolo Pino, not Ludovico Dolce as I had said, who first clearly divided the labor of the painter into the three categories of *disegno*, *inventione*, and *colorire*, which correspond to the three major divisions of the art of rhetoric among the ancients. In his brilliant book *Galileo as a Critic of the Arts* (The Hague, 1954), Erwin Panofsky's discussion of the great astronomer's contribution to the *paragone* literature is one that I should have liked to have at hand when I discussed Leonardo's *paragone*. For a number of the sixteenth-century treatises I discuss I refer the reader to the critical introductions, bibliography and notes in Paola Barocchi's *Trattati d'arte del cinquecento fra manierismo e controriforma*, Vols. 1 and 2 (Bari, 1960–62). Mark Roskill's new edition of Ludovico Dolce's *Dialogo della pittura*, which will shortly be published in the monograph series of the College Art Association of America and the Archaeological Institute of America, also contains valuable matter for the study of the humanistic theory of painting during the sixteenth century.

Rensselaer W. Lee

UT PICTURA POESIS

The Humanistic Theory of Painting

INTRODUCTION

TREATISES on art and literature written between the middle of the sixteenth and middle of the eighteenth century nearly always remark on the close relationship between painting and poetry.[1] The sister arts as they were generally called—and Lomazzo observes that they arrived at a single birth[2]—differed, it was acknowledged, in means and manner of expression, but were considered almost identical in fundamental nature, in content, and in purpose.[3] The saying attributed by Plutarch to Simonides that painting is mute poetry, poetry a speaking picture, was quoted frequently and with enthusiasm; and Horace's famous simile *ut pictura poesis*—as is painting so is poetry[4]—which the writers on art expected one to read "as is poetry so is painting,"[5] was invoked more and more as final sanction for a much closer relationship between the sister arts than Horace himself would probably have approved. So deeply rooted, in fact, was the association of painting with poetry that it is not unusual to find the critics referring in a way that startles the modern reader to poets as painters; and if they do not with equal bluntness call painters poets, at least they are almost unanimous in asserting that painting merits serious consideration as a liberal art only by virtue of its likeness to poetry. In the middle of the sixteenth century Ludovico Dolce is rather more inclusive than the average when he declares that not only poets, but all writers, are painters; that poetry, history, and in short, every composition of learned men (*qualunque componimento de'dotti*) is painting.[6]

1. In preparing this study I have been particularly indebted to Professor Erwin Panofsky for valuable advice and criticism. Professor Frank J. Mather, Jr., Professor Walter Friedlaender, and Professor Samuel H. Monk of the Department of English, Southwestern College, have also given useful suggestions. Mr Helmut von Erffa, Miss Margot Cutter, Mrs. Katharine Pediconi, and my wife have given generous assistance in various ways.

2. Giovanni Paolo Lomazzo, *Trattato dell'arte della pittura, scoltura, et architettura*, Milan, 1585, VI, 65, p. 486: "Considerando la cagione onde sia nato quel detto antico tanta esser la comfortità della Poesia con la pittura, che quasi nate ad un parto l'una pittura loquace e l'altra poesia mutola s'appellarono"; cf. Leonardo da Vinci, *Trattato della pittura*, ed. H. Ludwig, Vienna, 1872, I, 21, and see note 6.

3. This was also the opinion of antiquity: cf. Aristotle *Poetics* I–II. See also Plutarch *De gloria Atheniensium* III. 346 f–347 c, in which occurs the famous aphorism of Simonides that painting is mute poetry, poetry a speaking picture.

4. *Ars poetica* 361; see note 15 for the entire passage.

5. Charles du Fresnoy in his seventeenth-century poem *De arte graphica*, Paris, 1667, 1–8, so enjoins in a passage that remains the best single text for the entire doctrine based on *ut pictura poesis*, citing as it does both the Horatian simile and the saying of Simonides, and declaring in effect that painting, since unworthy subject matter concerns it no more than it does poetry, has an equal status with poetry as a liberal art:

"Ut pictura poesis erit; similisque Poesi

Sit Pictura; refert par aemula quaeque sororem,
Alternantque vices et nomina; muta Poesis
Dicitur haec, Pictura loquens solet illa vocari.
Quod fuit auditu gratum cecinere Poetae;
Quod pulchrum aspectu Pictores pingere curant:
Quaeque Poetarum Numeris indigna fuere,
Non eadem Pictorum Operam Studiumque merentur."

6. *Dialogo della pittura intitolato l'Aretino*, Florence, 1735 (first ed. Venice, 1557), p. 116. Dolce quotes as authority for his statement Petrarch's designation of Homer as "Primo pittor de le memorie antiche," and he explains what he means in another passage (pp. 106 ff.), when after stating that "il Pittore è intento a imitar per via di linee, e di colori . . . tutto quello che si dimostra all'occhio," he says that "il Poeta col mezzo delle parole va imitando non solo ciò che si dimostra all'occhio [here Dolce means he is like the painter], ma che ancora si rappresenta all'intelletto. Laonde essi in questo sono differenti, ma simili in tante altre parti, che si possono dir quasi fratelli." It was, then, in the imitation through the medium of words of that which the eye perceives in external nature that Dolce considered the poet to be like the painter whose media of imitation are lines and colors, though he legitimately added another province of the poet's art, the imitation of that "which is also represented to the intellect"—intellectual concepts and processes of thought—in which the painter does not share (see p. 60 and note 282): The concept allied to Dolce's that the poet, or for that matter the historian, is a painter in the sense that his descriptions have clearness or distinctness, is found in antiquity. Plutarch (*loc. cit.*)

Lomazzo not many years later, with an enthusiasm that even the sympathetic humanist will allow to be disproportionate to the truth, maintains the complementary view that there is no such thing as a painter (Lomazzo means a painter worthy of the name) who is not imbued with something of the poetic spirit.[7] And at the end of the critical tradition of the Renaissance Sir Joshua Reynolds can still refer quite naturally to Shakespeare as "that faithful and accurate painter of nature" or remark that "Michelangelo possessed the poetical part of our art in a most eminent degree."[8]

The habit of associating writers whose imagery is vivid or full of color with painters was known to antiquity.[9] Furthermore the critics of the sixteenth century had before their eyes in the unrivaled painting of the Renaissance an open book, so to speak, of brilliant pictorial imagery; and this fact, even without the encouragement of antiquity, might have made their references to certain poets as painters at once quite natural and a handsome compliment to the word-painting of the poets concerned. In any event, critics for two centuries believed that it was in pictorial vividness of representation, or, more accurately, of description—in the power to paint clear images of the external world in the mind's eye as a painter would record them on canvas—that the poet chiefly resembled the painter. Ariosto "when he marvelously describes the beauties of the fay Alcina" is for Dolce a painter who has provided those who paint on canvas with a perfect image of feminine beauty,[10] an opinion that finally in the mid-eighteenth century Lessing was not to share. For Lessing found in Ariosto's stanzas an excess of descriptive detail that resulted in no distinct image of a living woman and therefore overstepped the limits of the poet's art.[11] And the Laokoön was directed against those artistic transgressions, whether of poetry or the figure arts, that Horace's ut pictura poesis might encourage, or might be invoked to justify. With no more than this passing glance at the character and critical fortunes of poetry as the sister art of painting, and remembering Dolce's ominous qualification of painting as a learned art,

---

mentions this quality (ἐνάργεια) in Thucydides, and quotes from one of the historian's accounts of a battle to show that it is found both in the arrangement (διάθεσις) of the scene and in the writer's power of vivid description (διατύπωσις). Lucian (Εἰκόνες 8), anticipating Petrarch, calls Homer "the best of painters (τὸν ἄριστον τῶν γραφέων) even if Euphranor and Apelles are present," and suggests that the painter who would add color to the statue of ideal womanhood that he is imagining, remember Homer's description of Menelaus' thighs as ivory tinged with crimson, and his epithets of laughter-loving, white-armed, and rosy-fingered, all of which produce visual images in the mind's eye. On the antiquity of the concept of the poet as painter, and on the Renaissance and Baroque habit of calling poets painters and vice versa, see also the comments and citations in K. Borinski, Die Antike in Poetik und Kunsttheorie, Leipzig, 1914, I, 183ff. For the Renaissance conception of the poet as pictorial imagist see also the well-known passage in the second dialogue of Francisco de Hollanda (ed. J. de Vasconcellos, Vienna, 1899, p. 67) wherein Lattanzio remarks that "it would seem indeed that the poets had no other aim than to teach the excellence of painting . . . since one thing of which they are most studious is to paint well and imitate good painting." He then comments on the "paintings" of Virgil and observes that you may read all Virgil and discover nothing else therein but the art of a Michelangelo. It is Virgil's pictorial imagery that he has in mind—pastoral landscape, the harbor of Carthage surrounded by hills and woods, the burning of Troy, etc. Incidentally these Virgilian pictures that he cites are about as remote as possible from the painting of Michelangelo.

An interesting example, and more entertaining than most, of the habit common from the sixteenth to the eighteenth century of referring to poets as painters occurs in the painter Antoine Coypel's remark that Molière knew so well how to paint the characters of men that individuals have taken for their own portraits those that he made after general nature. Although there is here, no doubt, a certain confusion in Coypel's mind as to the capacities and limitations of painting and poetry, it is certainly Molière's ability to delineate character with objective vividness that leads Coypel to liken him to a painter. Coypel had previously remarked in a way that recalls Dolce that all which imitates nature is called painting, and that one is always calling Homer and Virgil great painters. No one who has read through much of the critical literature of the period will be inclined to disagree with this latter statement (see Coypel's discourses before the Académie Royale published in 1721, in H. Jouin, Conférences de l'Académie Royale de Peinture, Paris, 1883, p. 258). It is not difficult to see how this association of poetry with the painter's objective or vivid imitation of external nature could be put to bad uses in encouraging descriptive poetry. For some remarks on the influence of ut pictura poesis on the history of literature, see note 29.

7. Op. cit., VI, 2, p. 282.

8. Discourses VIII and XV. His fifteen Discourses were delivered before the Royal Academy from 1768 to 1790.

9. See note 6.

10. Op. cit., p. 178.

11. Laokoön, XX.

we may proceed to ask why the critics who named poets painters, also virtually identified the art of painting with the art of poetry.

Chiefly responsible without question was the authority of two ancient treatises on literature: Aristotle's *Poetics*, and Horace's *Ars poetica*. Both Aristotle and Horace had suggested interesting analogies between poetry and painting, though they had by no means tended to identify them as did the Renaissance and Baroque critics. Aristotle had said for instance that human nature in action is the object of imitation among painters as well as poets[12]—an analogy that was as true of Italian painting of the Renaissance as it had been of ancient painting; and in arguing that plot was the most essential element in tragedy he had remarked that a canvas smeared at random with the loveliest colors will not give as much pleasure as a portrait done in outline.[13] Thus plot in tragedy in a general way resembles design in painting, and the comparison is, it appears, innocent enough. But comparisons which to Aristotle were certainly no more than a means of clarifying his discourse on the drama served the critics as a point of departure for developing their often questionable doctrine of the sister arts. The *Ars poetica* provided two particularly potent texts for this doctrine. One was a passage in which Horace after describing a painting of grotesque hybrids and comparing it to a book whose vain imaginings are fashioned like a sick man's dreams, admits the equal right of painters and poets to liberty of imagination, provided this potentially dangerous Pegasus be tethered to the stall of the probable and congruous.[14] The other was the famous passage containing the simile *ut pictura poesis* in which the poet, after remarking that the sensible critic will know how to excuse the faults that must occur even in great literature, pleads for further flexibility in critical judgment by declaring in effect that poetry should be compared to painting which exhibits not merely a detailed style that requires close scrutiny, but also a broad, impressionistic style that will not please unless viewed from a distance.[15] Again these comparisons were in their place

12. *Poetics* II. 1: "'Επεὶ δὲ μιμοῦνται οἱ μιμούμενοι πράττον-τας'"—"since artists imitate men doing or experiencing something." Aristotle goes on to say that both poets and painters imitate men as better or worse than ourselves or much as we are, Polygnotus depicting them as better, Pauson as worse, and Dionysius like ourselves (cf. xxv. 26–28). This fundamental passage, often quoted or remembered by Renaissance and Baroque critics (cf. notes 41 and 64), was brought very much up to date in the early eighteenth century by Antoine Coypel who applied it not only to French classic drama (Corneille had made men better than they are, Racine as they are) but to the Florentine, Venetian, and Flemish schools of painting: Michelangelo and Raphael painted men better than they are "par la grandeur de leur goût et l'élévation de leurs idées" (one detects here the growing Longinian influence), Titian as they are; but the Flemings and Dutch "les ont fait plus méchants, c'est à dire par la bassesse des sujets et leur petit goût de dessin" (see Jouin, *op. cit.*, p. 249). Cf. note 52.

13. *Op. cit.* VI. 19–21: "'Αρχὴ μὲν οὖν καὶ οἷον ψυχὴ ὁ μῦθος τῆς τραγῳδίας, δεύτερον δὲ τὰ ἤθη. παραπλήσιον γάρ ἐστιν καὶ ἐπὶ τῆς γραφικῆς. εἰ γάρ τις ἐναλείψειε τοῖς καλλίστοις φαρμάκοις χύδην, οὐκ ἂν ὁμοίως εὐφράνειεν καὶ λευκογραφήσας εἰκόνα."

14. *Ars poetica* 1–13:
"Humano capiti cervicem pictor equinam iungere si velit, et varias inducere plumas undique collatis membris, ut turpiter atrum desinat in piscem mulier formosa superne, spectatum admissi risum teneatis, amici? credite, Pisones, isti tabulae fore librum persimilem, cuius, velut aegri somnia, vanae

fingentur species, ut nec pes nec caput uni reddatur formae. 'pictoribus atque poetis quidlibet audendi semper fuit aequa potestas.' scimus, et hanc veniam petimusque damusque vicissim; sed non ut placidis coeant immitia, non ut serpentes avibus geminentur, tigribus agni."

As early as the thirteenth century Durandus with Horace in mind had already sanctioned the painter's freedom of imagination. Cennini in his *Libro dell'arte* (ed. Milanesi, Florence, 1859, p. 2) had compared poet and painter in a manner similar to Horace. Speaking of painting as coming next in honor after science, he remarks: "E con ragione merita metterla a sedere in secondo grado alla scienza, e coronarla di poesia. La ragione è questa: che il poeta, con la scienza prima che ha, il fa degno e libero di poter comporre e legare insieme sì e no come gli piace, secondo sua volontà. Per lo simile al dipintore dato è libertà potere comporre una figura ritta, a sedere, mezzo uomo, mezzo cavallo, si come gli piace, secondo sua fantasia." But with the grotesquerie of medieval art behind him, Cennini does not include Horace's deprecation of art that is "velut aegri somnia." For Durandus and Cennini see Borinski, *op. cit.*, I, 96–97. Cennini's coupling of painting with poetry on grounds of imaginative freedom is an interesting anticipation of many passages in sixteenth- and seventeenth-century criticism. See notes 145, 171.

15. *Ibid.* 361–365:
"Ut pictura poesis: erit quae, si propius stes, te capiat magis, et quaedam, si longius abstes. haec amat obscurum, volet haec sub luce videri, iudicis argutum quae non formidat acumen; haec placuit semel, haec deciens repetita placebit."

legitimate and illuminating, but when they were appropriated by the Renaissance en-
thusiasts who sought for painting the honors long accorded poetry, their original context
was not always remembered.

The Renaissance champions of painting who proclaimed its noble rank among the arts,
and in the famous case of Leonardo da Vinci its superiority even to poetry,[16] were until
the sixteenth century more generally concerned with the technical problems and scientific
theory of their art than with the development of a fundamental aesthetic. Their foremost interest, and this reflected, of course, the realistic development of painting during
the Quattrocento, was in how the painter might represent in its completeness the three-
dimensional world on a two-dimensional surface. When, however, the progress of realistic
experiment had ended for the time being, and after the brief glory of the high Renaissance
in Florence and Rome, painting had settled into the uncreative formulas of Mannerism,
criticism in a way that recalls its rise under not dissimilar conditions in fourth-century
Greece, took a new lease on life. But towards the end of the sixteenth century the painter-
theorists like Lomazzo and Armenini were no longer concerned, as Leonardo had been,
with recording new technical or scientific knowledge based on actual experiment in painting.[17] Instead they were interested in organizing and codifying knowledge already at
hand for the benefit of young painters who all the more, it was believed, because they lived
in a degenerate age, needed categorical instruction based on the great invention and
practice of the past;[18] for the critics of painting no less than the nostalgic poets of the
time looked backward wistfully to the golden age of ancient art, and with excellent reasons
of their own to the recent triumphs of the Renaissance.[19] They had the professional point
of view of an age of academicians, including the naive belief that prescription literally
followed insures good practice.

The codifying of technical and scientific knowledge was, however, only one aspect of
the new criticism and historically the least important. For after 1550 all critics whether
painters or not—and here again theory intervened to assert ideal potentialities of the art
that were no longer evident in its practice—were concerned with defining painting in
fundamental terms; and this included, as was remarked above, a discussion of its essential
nature, its content, and its end. In this philosophical province it was natural, even obliga-
tory since the critics lived under the always lengthening shadow of Greece and Rome, that
they should turn like the critics of literature to the authority of antiquity. But no theoretical treatise had survived that attempted, as the *Poetics* did for literature, to define the
nature of the art of painting, and to discuss it in terms of formal aesthetic; nor had the
Renaissance inherited any seasoned advice to the practicing painter concerning good taste
or effective presentation that could compare with the shrewd good sense and practical wisdom of the *Ars poetica*.[20] Now the analogies between poetry and painting that these famous

---

16. For Leonardo's comparison of painting with poetry
see his *Trattato della pittura*, I, 2, 14–28, 46. These passages
are brought together and translated in J. P. Richter, *The
Literary Works of Leonardo da Vinci*, 2nd ed., London,
1939, I, 52–68.

17. See the chapter on the theory of art in the period of
Mannerism in J. Schlosser-Magnino, *La letteratura artistica*,
Florence, 1939, pp. 332–51.

18. For Lomazzo this knowledge was not only the technical and scientific knowledge that concerned proportion,
movement, color, light, and perspective—the subjects of the
first five books of the *Trattato*—but also the knowledge
based on ancient and modern literature and the history of
painting and sculpture that would help to insure an expres-

sive and appropriate composition for a vast variety of subjects (book VI); and the knowledge of iconography in the
narrower sense—attributes of the Trinity, saints, pagan
gods, etc. (book VII). See especially *Trattato*, "Proemio,"
pp. 11–16; cf. Gio. Battista Armenini, *De' veri precetti della
pittura*, Pisa, 1821 (first ed. Ravenna, 1587), I, I, pp. 13 ff.;
cf. also the second paragraph in Appendix I.

19. See Lomazzo, *op. cit.*, VI, 64, p. 481.

20. Roger de Piles in his comparison of painting and
poetry (*Cours de peinture*, Paris, 1708, pp. 420 ff.) was well
aware of the fact that little valuable criticism of painting
and little painting of value had survived from antiquity,
and he regarded it as prejudicial to the esteem in which
painting was held by many sensible people of his day—

treatises contained could not fail in a humanistic age to impress critics who sought to invest painting with the dignity of a liberal art, for Aristotle and Horace, not to mention fragmentary utterances of other ancient writers,[21] had by implication already accorded her this dignity. And being in search of the doctrine that these ancient analogies seemed to imply, and finding it nowhere developed in antiquity,[22] the critics did not limit their borrowings from the *Poetics* and the *Ars poetica* to those passages, after all few in number, in which painting and poetry are compared. Far more important, they did not hesitate to appropriate as the foundation of their own theory many basic concepts of the two ancient treatises, making them apply in a more or less Procrustean manner to the art of painting for which they were never intended. The theory of painting that resulted could not fail under such conditions to show much that was pedantic and absurd if it was not absolutely false, for in imposing on painting what was merely a reconditioned theory of poetry, the enthusiastic critics did not stop to ask whether an art with a different medium could reasonably submit to a borrowed aesthetic. And it was when the critics were occasionally independent enough to stray from the beaten path of antique doctrine, and, instead of harping on the obvious likenesses of painting and poetry, attempted to analyze their differences or engaged in lively apology for one art or the other, that their remarks were often the most illuminating. Nevertheless the new *Ars pictoria* for all its defects was the child of the humanistic Renaissance, and contained much that was reasonable and true—much, indeed, that is so obviously true that even the sympathetic reader of sixteenth-century treatises is both vexed and amazed at the repetitious verbosity which attended the humanistic investiture of the art of painting. And the core of the new as of the ancient theory—that painting like poetry fulfils its highest function in a representative imitation of human life, not in its average but in its superior forms—is, notwithstanding its virtual eclipse at the present time, important and central to any final estimate of the painter's art.

This humanistic doctrine had been more than implied, if never clearly defined, a century before the age of criticism began in Italy, in the writing of Leon Battista Alberti,[23] who, though unfamiliar with Aristotle's *Poetics*, knew that the painting of a "history"—a significant human action—is the chief business of a serious painter, and had learned from Latin authors that the artists of antiquity had sought to bestow an ideal beauty upon their works. It appears later in the treatise of Leonardo,[24] for if the experimental painter-scientist was largely unconcerned with inherited theory, he still could not fail to absorb some of it in the intellectual air of Florence; and Leonardo further shows the inalienable humanism of his race in his famous and often repeated statement that the expression of human emo-

---

people who obviously set great store by the prestige afforded by antique models. See Appendix I, "On the Lack of Ancient Criticism of Painting."

21. Plutarch, for instance, says that painters and poets represent the same subjects, and that the underlying purpose of both is the same (*De gloria Atheniensium* III. 347*a*); the elder Philostratus finds painting and poetry equally the repositories of wisdom (*Imagines* I. 294*k*); the younger Philostratus emphasizes the power of painting to express character and emotion and finds a certain element of imagination (φαντασία) common to painting and dramatic poetry (*Imagines*, Procemium, 390*k*).

22. Pliny's famous account of painting in antiquity (*Historia naturalis* xxxv) upon which the sixteenth-century critics drew so heavily in their desire to proclaim the time-honored dignity of the art, although it occasionally adumbrates theories of art, is not a theoretical work.

23. *Della pittura*, 1436. See the standard edition of Janitschek, *L. B. Alberti's kleinere kunsttheoretische Schriften*, Vienna, 1877, pp. 143 ff. Cf. Cicero *De inventione* II. 1, 1; *Orator ad Brutum* II. 7 ff., where the theory of ideal imitation has a strongly Platonic rather than Aristotelian character; Pliny *op. cit.* 62–64; notes 50, 69, 74, 97. Aristotle's *Poetics* was not well known until the sixteenth century. The first reliable Latin translation, that of Giorgio Valla, appeared in 1498; the first commentary, Robortelli's, in 1548; the first Italian translation, Segni's, in 1549. Both Robortelli and Segni remark on the long neglect of the book. See J. E. Spingarn, *A History of Literary Criticism in the Renaissance*, 7th impression, New York, 1938, pp. 16 ff.

24. In his admonition to the painter "to be solitary and consider what he sees and discuss with himself, choosing the most excellent parts of the species of whatever he sees." "If he does this," Leonardo adds, "he will appear to be a second nature." See *Trattato*, I, 58*a*.

tion through bodily movement is fundamental to the painter's art.[25] Most significant of all
—and one will make due allowance for important differences in conception and expression
between the art of antiquity and that of the Renaissance—the doctrine of ideal imitation
had been essentially embodied in the greatest Italian painting from Cimabue to Michelangelo. It could not, then, fail to be axiomatic in a consciously critical age like the later-
sixteenth century that, despite its spiritual confusion and its pedantry, still nourished the
flame of humanism, and that possessed so magnificent an inheritance, both distant and
immediate, of mythopoetic art. The seventeenth century continued to cherish the humanistic theory of painting and developed it, moreover, in a way that the preceding century
had never done. For the Italian critics, intent on the more important business of pointing
out how painting resembled poetry in range and profundity of content, or in power of
expression, had never fostered the notion, though it could be traced back to Aristotle, of
purely formal correspondences between the sister arts: design equals plot, color equals
words, and the like.[26] But the later French and English critics sometimes overworked these
correspondences,[27] and by what amounted to a most unfortunate extension of the same
kind of artificial parallel, they sometimes attempted to enclose the art of painting in an
Aristotelian strait-jacket of dramatic theory.[28] The result for criticism and practice was a
serious confusion of the arts that resulted, as every one knows, in Lessing's vigorous and
timely attempt in the mid-eighteenth century to redefine poetry and painting and to assign
to each its proper boundaries.[29] In the preceding century, in fact, La Fontaine neatly

25. *Ibid.*, 122, 483, etc.

26. See note 13. Cicero (*Orator* XIX. 65) had compared
the Sophists' use of words to a painter's arrangement of
colors. Plutarch in a curious passage (*Moralia* 16c) compares color which "is more stimulating than line drawing
because it is life-like and creates an illusion" with plausible
fiction; line is by implication compared with a work of
literature that lacks the illusion of life even though it be
elaborate in meter and diction. This is a very unusual
parallel and does not recur, so far as I know, in later criticism. It would have pleased the "Rubenistes" at the close
of the seventeenth century. Cf. note 41.

27. John Dryden, for instance, for whom in the usual
manner plot equals design and "Expression, and all that
belongs to Words, is that in a Poem, which Colouring is in
a Picture," after making some remarks on design and color
in the ancient poets (e.g. Virgil's design is inferior to
Homer's, but his coloring better) goes on to say that lights
and shadows are like tropes and figures. The whole comparison, which extends for several pages, is absurdly elaborate (see his *Parallel between Painting and Poetry*, the
preface to his translation of Du Fresnoy, London, 1716, p.
LI ff.; first ed. 1695).

The Abbé Batteaux remarks that "les mesures et l'har-
monie" constitute the coloring of poetry, imitation its design (*Les beaux arts réduits à un même principe*, Paris, 1746,
pp. 138, 140). Elsewhere in the same essay he says what
amounts to the same thing when he equates "desseing"
with "fable," "coloris" with "versification" (p. 247). When
Minturno in the sixteenth century differentiates the means
of imitation in poetry from those in painting, he is not concerned as Dryden and Batteaux were, in establishing formal
correspondences between them (see note 41).

28. See pp. 62 ff. below.

29. For the effect of the doctrine *ut pictura poesis* on
literature during the seventeenth and eighteenth centuries
see pp. 3–57 of the late Professor Irving Babbitt's essay
The New Laokoön, Boston and New York, 1910, which
deserves to be better known among historians of art.
Babbitt shows clearly how the formal confusion of the arts

engendered by *ut pictura poesis* led first in the seventeenth
century, under the influence of the pseudo-Aristotelian
doctrine of the Renaissance that it was better to imitate
the ancients than real life, to the use of "poetical diction"
—that stock of traditional words, elegant phrases, figures
of speech and the like, known as the poetical colors (as
opposed to choice of subject and mode of treatment which
were compared to design in the sense of an outline drawing
or sketch) that the poet was supposed to lay on from the
outside like pigments. Such a theory of poetry could only
result in that extreme artificiality of language against
which the Romantic poets revolted in the name of spontane-
ous and sincere expression.

The school of descriptive poetry that arose in the first
half of the eighteenth century as a result of the growing
interest in external nature and found in Thomson's *Seasons*
its finest and most influential example, showed a new
capacity on the part of the poets for writing with their eyes
on the object, rather than on literary models, although
even the best of them are never free from the influences of
poetical diction. This school was quick to enlist under the
banner of *ut pictura poesis* in order to justify its own kind
of poetical pictures: descriptions, often exhaustive, of
landscape, rustic life, still-life including farm equipment,
etc.; and it was against this school, strongly represented in
Germany by Brockes, Haller, and Kleist, that Lessing
revolted both as a humanist and as an aesthetician, believing as he did that the medium of poetry is fundamentally
adapted to the rendering of human action, not to description; for words that follow one another in time can only
produce, in the successive addition of details in a description, a blurred and confused image, whereas the painter
can render these details as they coexist in space and produce
a clear image that can be apprehended in a single moment of
time (*Laokoön*, XVI–XX). For a useful and fairly complete
summary of critical opinions concerning the relationship
between painting and poetry up to Lessing's time, see
W. G. Howard's introduction to his edition of the *Laokoön*,
New York, 1910; for a more extended, though not very
conclusive, study of how the critics of painting interpreted

anticipating Lessing had already put his finger at the root of the trouble when he wrote:

> Les mots et les couleurs ne sont choses pareilles
> Ni les yeux ne sont les oreilles.[30]

I—IMITATION

This essay will first attempt to sketch the development of the humanistic theory of painting in European criticism of the sixteenth and seventeenth centuries, noting how it is everywhere pervaded and molded by the direct or implied comparison of painting with poetry; it will then test one aspect of the theory by applying it to a capital example in the Baroque period of the impact of poetry on the sister art—the illustration of a famous episode of Tasso's *Gerusalemme liberata* among the painters of the seventeenth century. Inasmuch as the doctrine of imitation was the corner-stone of Renaissance as it had been of ancient aesthetic, one may reasonably begin a discussion entitled *ut pictura poesis* with a consideration of the manner in which the Italian critics of the sixteenth century applied to the art of painting a doctrine which the ancients had developed chiefly as it concerned the art of literature.

First of all, the critics observed in language unmistakably Aristotelian that painting like poetry was an imitation of nature, by which they meant human nature, and human nature not as it is, but, in Aristotle's phrase, as it ought to be,[31] "raised," as a modern writer has well expressed it, "above all that is local and accidental, purged of all that is abnormal and eccentric, so as to be in the highest sense representative."[32] In the sixteenth century the doctrine of ideal imitation had not yet entirely supplanted the older and scarcely compatible notion that art is an exact imitation of nature, and it is not unusual, at least until past the middle of the century, to find them disconcertingly side by side—a fact which, the reader will agree, does not argue for the philosophical capacities of these writers. The concept of literal imitation had occurred already in the Trecento,[33] and was the natural accompaniment during the Quattrocento of a realistic point of view and practice among those artists who were striving strenuously to capture the perfect illusion of visible

---

this relationship, see his *"Ut pictura poesis"* in *Publ. of the Mod. Lang. Assn. of America*, XXIV, 1909, 40–123. Howard has availed himself of the learned introduction and commentary in Hugo Blümner's monumental edition of the *Laokoön*, Berlin, 1880.

30. *Conte du Tableau*. Various writers have called attention to La Fontaine's anticipation of Lessing.

31. See especially the famous passage (*Poetics* IX. 1–3) where Aristotle states that poetry is more philosophic and serious than history because it reveals general truths, whereas history gives only particular facts; and cf. XV. 11 (see Bellori's translation below, note 64) and XXV. 1–2. The literary theorists of the Cinquecento frequently remark that poetry is like painting in its power to idealize nature. Fracastoro (*Naugerius sive de poetica dialogus*, Venice, 1555; I quote from the text reprinted by Ruth Kelso in *University of Illinois Studies in Language and Literature*, IX, 1924, p. 158) remembering Plato and Aristotle, states that the poet is not like the realistic painter who paints things as they are, but like the painter who contemplating the most fair and universal idea of his creator fashions them as they ought to be: "Video, o amici, in paucissimis illis tanti philosophi verbis illuscere ac patefieri nobis

poetae officium ac finem: alii siquidem singulare ipsum considerant, poeta vero universale, quasi alii similes sint illi pictori, qui et vultus et reliqua membra imitatur, qualia prorsus in re sunt, poeta vero illi adsimiletur qui non hunc, non illum vult imitari, non uti sorte sunt et defectus multos sustinent, sed universalem, et pulcherrimam ideam artificis sui contemplatus res facit, quales esse deceret." In like manner Scaliger compares Virgil, for him the paragon among ancient poets, with those painters and sculptors who, selecting the best from many objects in nature and combining these excellences into one image, seem "not to have learned from nature, but to have vied with her, or rather to have created laws for her to obey" (*Poetices*, Geneva, 1561, III, 25, p. 113). The passage is quoted and receives further comment in note 43. For a general survey of the theory of poetry during the Renaissance which it may be useful to compare with my discussion of the literary theory of painting, see Spingarn's *Literary Criticism in the Renaissance*, especially pp. 3–59.

32. Quoted from Babbitt, *op. cit.*, p. 10.

33. For instance in Boccaccio's praise of Giotto's ability to paint so accurate a likeness of things that men mistook his paintings for reality; see *Decameron*, VI, 5. This recalls Pliny.

nature.[34] Furthermore, it had received a kind of blessing from antiquity in Pliny's account of those ancient painters who created so convincing an illusion of life that animals and men, nay artists themselves, mistook their art for reality.[35] Leonardo at the crossroads between the early and high Renaissance knew, for all his intense interest in the particular, that painting is a great deal more than literal representation,[36] yet he could also remark that a picture is most praiseworthy when it conforms most to the thing imitated;[37] and although Vasari in his attempt at a theoretical introduction to the art of painting shows that he is aware of the universalizing function of art,[38] the *Lives* are filled, as everyone knows, with an admiration of literal imitation that sometimes rivals Pliny; and he even praises Raphael, purest type of the high Renaissance style, for his unsurpassed naturalism. No one can doubt then that as late as the mid-sixteenth century cultivated men, with a genial inconsistency that would give pause to any thoroughgoing theoretician, could adopt the current idea of art as a generalizing and embellishing agent, yet still consider the painter's ability to be the ape of nature—the *scimmia della natura*—his foremost accomplishment. Greater consistency, indeed, might be expected of the critic Dolce, author of the first notable humanistic treatise on painting in the Cinquecento, for he was steeped in the ancient theoreticians as Leonardo and Vasari who had more compelling interests were not, and had published in his youth a translation of Horace's *Ars poetica*. Yet even Dolce, after defining art as the imitation of nature, and adding that the painter whose works most nearly approach her is the most perfect master,[39] can in a later passage redefine the goal of art by remarking that "the painter must labor hard not only to imitate but also to surpass nature."[40] Dolce was probably aware of inconsistency, for he tries to square the first definition with the second by insisting that it is only in creating the human figure that the painter

34. Alberti, whose theory in many respects anticipates the Cinquecento, nevertheless states that it is the painter's business to reproduce reality very closely (*Della pittura*, p. 143); and his instructions concerning perspective and anatomy belong to an age that was scientifically interested in the exact reproduction of reality.

35. *Hist. nat.* XXXV.

36. See note 24.

37. *Trattato*, III, 411.

38. Introduction to the 1568 edition of the *Vite* (ed. Milanesi, Florence, 1878, pp. 168 ff.). Vasari was elsewhere aware of the idealizing function of art. See Schlosser-Magnino, *La letteratura artistica*, pp. 278 ff.

39. *Dialogo della pittura*, p. 106: "Dico . . . la Pittura non essere altro che imitatione della Natura: e colui, che più nelle sue opere le si avicina, è più perfetto Maestro." Cf. p. 112.

40. *Ibid.*, p. 176: "Deve adunque il Pittore procacciar non solo d'imitar, ma di superar la natura. Dico superar la Natura in una parte: che nel resto è miraculoso, non pur, se vi arriva, ma quando vi si avicina. Questo è in dimostrar col mezzo dell'arte in un corpo solo tutta quella perfettion di bellezza, che la natura non suol dimostrare a pena in mille. Perchè non si trova un corpo humano così perfettamente bello, che non gli manchi alcuna parte. Onde habbiamo esempio di Zeusi . . ." (the story of Zeuxis follows). Dolce here anticipates in a tentative and unsystematic way, and without discarding the really antagonistic theory of the direct imitation of nature, Bellori's seventeenth-century Platonico-Aristotelian definition of art (see p. 14 and notes 55-60) as the artist's imitation of an Idea or mental image of beauty in his own mind derived, as in the case of Zeuxis, from a bringing together of excellences observed in different individuals none of whom was, however, perfectly beautiful in himself. Dolce, who was anything but a systematic thinker, thus reflects in unreconciled

form opposite points of view concerning imitation that had been present in antiquity itself (see E. Panofsky, *Idea*, Leipzig, 1924, pp. 5 ff., for discussion of antique theories of imitation). He was still too close to the realistic point of view of the Renaissance to give up entirely, as Bellori did later, the theory of exact imitation of nature in favor of the definite theory of art as a universalizing and embellishing agent. In an interesting passage in Benedetto Varchi (*Due lezzioni*, Florence, 1549, pp. 111 ff.), Dolce could have found a hint for his juxtaposition of the two doctrines of imitation. Apropos of the fact that poets and painters have a like goal in imitating nature (cf. note 6 for Dolce's comments on the same subject), Varchi writes: "Essendo il fine della Poesia e della Pittura il Medesimo, secondo alcuni, *cioè imitare la natura, quanto possono il piu*, vengono ad essere una medesima, e nobili ad un modo, e però molte volte gli scrittori danno a' Pittori quello, che è de' Poeti, e cosi per lo contrario, onde Dante, che . . . seppe tutto, e tutto scrisse, pose nel Ventinovesimo canto del Purgatorio: 'Ma legge Ezechiel, che gli dipinse.'" Varchi here states the Renaissance doctrine already noted in Dolce of the exact imitation of nature. But shortly after he continues: "I dipintori, se bene nel ritrarre dal naturale, debbono imitare la natura, e sprimere il vero quanto piu fanno, *possono non dimeno, anzi debbono, come ancora i Poeti, usare alcuna discrezione*, onde molto fu lodato la prudenza d'Apelle, il quale devendo ritrarre Antigono, che era cieco da uno occhio diede tal sito alla figura, che ascose quell'occhio di maniera, che non si poteva vedere." Here Varchi qualifies his advice to the painter to imitate nature as closely as possible with the phrase *con alcuna discrezione*, a phrase which hints at idealization and which he explains in the familiar story of Apelles and Antigonus; and he thus closely parallels Dolce who, though he advises painters to imitate nature exactly, says that art must at the same time surpass nature.

may improve upon nature; in all other respects he is hopelessly outclassed. The old notion of exact imitation Dolce can still accept with some enthusiasm for nature in general, but for the all-important human figure to which in Italian painting the rest of nature had always been subsidiary, it will no longer do. And it is apropos of the human figure in action that Dolce, following the method of literary critics of his day who were prescribing rules for poetry based on Aristotle and Horace,[41] developed his own doctrine of ideal imitation. It will be worth while briefly to examine his treatment of the doctrine, for it contains, though in attenuated and undeveloped form, most of the fundamentals of an aesthetic theory that will persist for two centuries.

Dolce discusses two ways whereby the painter may, to repeat Aristotle's phrase, represent life not as it is, but as it ought to be. By a method which Aristotle would have approved, he may go direct to nature, and selecting the fairest parts from a number of individuals, produce a composite figure more perfect than commonly exists. This was the celebrated method of Zeuxis in painting the divine beauty of Helen, and one that few writers on painting after Alberti ever forgot to extol.[42] Or he may use as perfect a single model as he can find, following the example of Apelles and Praxiteles who rendered their celebrated images of Aphrodite after Phryne, most beautiful of courtesans. Now in the golden age of antiquity an Apelles who had a Phryne for a model could succeed by this really unorthodox method. But a modern artist, Dolce insists, cannot find a standard of perfection in a single woman, for nature even under the best conditions is never without her defects. If then the artist, correcting her imperfections, would "surpass nature," would render her fairer than she is, he must be guided by a study of the faultless antique. For the antique is already that ideal nature for which the painter strives and "the ancient statues contain all the perfection of art."[43]

41. The most important sixteenth-century treatises on poetry were the following: Vida, *De arte poetica*, Rome, 1527 (in verse); Daniello, *La poetica*, Venice, 1536; Robortelli, *In librum Aristotelis de arte poetica explicationes*, Florence, 1548; Fracastoro, *Naugerius sive de poetica dialogus*, Venice, 1555; Minturno, *De poeta*, Venice, 1559, and *L'arte poetica*, Venice, 1564; J. C. Scaliger, *Poetices*, Geneva, 1561; Castelvetro, *La poetica d'Aristotele, vulgarizzata et sposta*, Vienna, 1570; Torquato Tasso, *Discorsi dell'arte poetica*, Venice, 1587. All of the comparisons between painting and poetry in Aristotle and Horace were also available to the critics of painting in these influential treatises where they recur many times. The following, for instance, is Minturno's way of summing up Aristotle's position that poetry and painting have the same objects of imitation, but that their means of imitation are different: "Ne più la poesia, che la pittura questa varietà di persone ci discrive [Minturno has just been saying that poets represent men as better or worse than they are, or as average]. Perciochè tra pittori Polygnoto i migliori dipinse; Pausone i peggiori; Dionysio i mezzani. Diverse anchora sono le cose con le quali si fa l'imitazione. Conciosia cosa che i pittori con li colori e co' liniamenti la facciano: ... i poeti, com' ho detto, con le parole, con l'harmonia, con li tempi" (*L'arte poetica*, pp. 2–3). Cf. notes 12, 13, 26, 27.

42. See note 40.

43. *Op. cit.*, p. 190: "Devesi adunque elegger la forma più perfetta, imitando parte la Natura. Il che faceva Apelle, il quale ritrasse la sua tanto celebrata Venere, che usciva dal Mare ... da Frine famosissima cortigiana della sua età; et ancora Prasitele cavò la bella statua della Venere Gnidia della medesima giovane. E parte si debbono imitar le belle figure di marmo, o di bronzo de' Mestieri antichi. La mirabil perfettion delle quali chi gusterà e possederà a

pieno, potrà sicuramente corregger molti difetti di essa Natura, e far le sue Pitture riguardevoli e grate a ciascuno: *perciochè le cose antiche contengono tutta la perfettion dell'arte, e possono essere esemplari di tutto il bello.*" For Scaliger, Virgil among ancient poets was superior to nature for the same reasons that Dolce found the ancient artists superior. The following passage (*Poetices*, III, 25, p. 113) which should also be compared with the quotation from Dolce in note 40, is a most interesting epitome of what was most important in Renaissance æsthetic combining as it does the comparison of Virgil to painters who idealize nature; the doctrine that by a selective process the painter is able, as Dolce said, "non solo d'imitar, ma di superar la natura"; the doctrine that there is a universal perfection inherent in the regular system of proportions in nature (cf. Vasari, *loc. cit.* in note 38), but that nature contains defects which result from accidents of time and place; finally the notion that antiquity is "belle nature": "Hactenus rerum ideae quem ad modum ex ipsa natura exciperentur, Virgilianis ostendimus exemplis. Ita enim eius poesi evenisse censeo sicut et picturis. Nam et plastae et ii, qui coloribus utuntur, ex ipsis rebus capessunt notiones, quibus lineamenta, lucem, umbram, recessus imitentur. Quod in quibusque praestantissimum inveniunt, e multis in unum opus suum transferunt: ita ut non a natura didicisse, sed cum ea certasse, aut potius illi dare leges potuisse videantur Quis enim putet ullam unquam talem fuisse foeminae cuiuspiam pulchritudinem in qua aliquid non desideraretur ab iudice non vulgari? Nam tametsi in ipsis naturae normis atque dimensionibus universa perfectio est: tamen utriusque parentis mistio, tempus, coelum, locus multa afferunt impedimenta. Itaque non ex ipsius naturae opere uno potuimus exempla capere, quae ex una Virgiliana idea mutuati sumus."

It is noteworthy that when Dolce counsels the painter to imitate "le belle figure di marmo o di bronzo de' Mestieri antichi," he does not think of such imitation as an end in itself, but as a means to an end. And if, we may surmise, the painter did not fall into the aesthetic quagmire of merely copying the antique statues, but used them discreetly as a criterion of ideal attainment, he might as successfully achieve that higher beauty for which he strove as if he had followed the first and less precarious method for the creative artist of "improving upon nature with means drawn from nature herself" without having dangerous recourse to the perfect standards of ancient art. Dolce does not say that one method is better than the other, and he would probably have agreed that a good artist could success-fully combine the selective imitation of nature with intelligent adaptations from the antique. But any student of Renaissance theory knows into what a cul-de-sac of criticism the literary theorists often strayed in their exaggerated admiration of antiquity, and how the deeper implications of Aristotle's doctrine were often lost in the constant admonition to the poets to imitate ancient models.[44] Now Horace, whose authority in the sixteenth century was enormous, had pointed out the way to this modification of the Aristotelian doctrine in urging his dramatic poet to be chary of new invention and follow, instead, the *exemplaria Graeca*—to find a model, that is, in the great poetry of the past.[45] And without this hint from Horace or some other Latin admirer of Greek forbears, ancient art and literature in the sixteenth century commanded sufficient admiration to have generated of themselves the pseudo-Aristotelian doctrine of the imitation of perfect models. Fortunately throughout the tradition of classicism in Renaissance and Baroque criticism the critics of painting generally succeeded, as Dolce did, in preserving more of Aristotle's meaning than the literary theorists,[46] but the pseudo-Aristotelian doctrine of imitation was always potentially dangerous, and among the French Academicians of the seventeenth century was strong enough to encourage the production of a kind of art that only the deeper understanding of a Poussin could save from empty formalism.[47] For the advice to follow the antique, or perhaps an exemplary modern like Raphael who had shown the way to its successful imitation, always tended to become a dogmatic counsel to abide by an artificial and forever invariable canon of beauty. And, if accepted in any sense literally, such counsel could only result in that uninspired traditionalism against which the Romantic Movement in the name of individual expression and a fresh interest in particular nature would finally revolt.

---

44. Scaliger, for instance, following Vida, carried the un-Aristotelian notion of the imitation of models to a dog-matic extreme in practically deifying Virgil. Why bother with nature at all, he says, when you have everything you may want to imitate in Virgil who is a second nature (*Poetices*, III, 4, p. 86). Later he added, apparently with some heat (*ibid.*, v, 3, p. 233), that "nothing was omitted by that heavenly genius: there is nothing to be added un-less by fools, nothing to be changed unless by the impu-dent." (*Ita nihil omissum coelesti viro illi: nihil addendum, nisi ab ineptis, nihil immutandum nisi ab impudentibus.*) Cf. Pope's remark in the *Essay on Criticism* that Virgil had found his own second nature in Homer:

"But when t'examine ev'ry part he came,
Nature and Homer were, he found, the same."

See the discussion of the theory of imitation in Babbitt, *The New Laokoön*, pp. 3–18.

45. See note 68.

46. At the end of the seventeenth century Roger de Piles sums up at its best the critical attitude toward the study of antiquity, adding a particular word of caution for the painter who in imitating ancient sculpture would be imitat-ing an art different in certain ways from his own: "Le Peintre ne sauroit donc mieux faire que de tâcher à pénétrer l'excellence de ces Ouvrages, pour connoître la pureté de la Nature, et pour dessiner plus doctement et plus élé-gamment. Néanmoins comme il y a dans la Sculpture plusieurs choses qui ne conviennent point à la Peinture et que le Peintre a d'ailleurs des moyens d'imiter la Nature plus parfaitement que le Sculpteur, il faut qu'il regarde l'Antique comme un Livre qu'on a traduit dans une autre langue, dans laquelle il suffit de bien rapporter le sens et l'esprit, sans s'attacher servilement aux paroles de l'Origi-nal" ("L'idée du peintre parfait" in his *Abrégé de la vie des peintres*, Paris, 1715, pp. 26–27; 1st ed. 1699).

47. See Félibien's report of Van Opstal's analysis of the Laokoön group before the Académie Royale de Peinture et de Sculpture; also Sébastien Bourdon's remarks on the imitation of antique statues (Jouin, *Conférences de l'Acad-émie*, pp. 19–26; 137–40). These are exaggerated examples of the uncritical worship of the antique. Bourdon's own painting is, in part at least, typical of the stultifying effect of such doctrine. In condemning the Academy's excessive enthusiasm for antique models, it should not be forgotten that some sensible things were said during its *Conférences*.

The cult of the antique produced then in the sixteenth century an important modification of Aristotle's theory of imitation that had far-reaching results. For Aristotle himself had not counseled the imitation of models, but clearly believed that significant imitation of nature is a function of the selective imagination and does not fundamentally depend on any external norm of perfection like the antique. Nor did Aristotle in his profound doctrine of the imitation of a superior nature mean that the artist should turn from nature herself, who must always provide fresh materials for selective imitation, to an a priori Idea of perfection in his own mind. But near the end of the century a Neo-Platonic critic like Lomazzo could temporarily divert the theory of imitation entirely from Aristotelian channels by declaring that ideal beauty, the image of which one sees reflected in the mirror of his own mind, has its source in God rather than in nature—a quasi-religious and mystical doctrine in harmony with the serious temper of the Counter-Reform, and one that did not empirically find a standard of excellence in selecting the best from concrete and external nature, but discovered it in Platonic fashion in the subjective contemplation of an inward, immaterial Idea.[48] But in 1664, in the secularizing age of the high Baroque, Giovanni Pietro Bellori resumed and brought to fruition what had been until the late sixteenth century the normal Italian mode of thinking about the arts.[49] Before Bellori wrote, this habit of mind, by nature empirical yet possessing a deep, qualifying strain of idealism, had found in the realm of aesthetic philosophy only hesitant and tentative expression. Alberti and Vasari, and one may include Raphael in a famous letter to Castiglione, had all associated the Idea that raises art above the mere imitation of things with direct experience of nature;[50] but their utterances on the subject are naive or fragmentary, and are valuable less as contributions to aesthetic than as interesting reactions of a receptive and sensitive artist and of two distinguished writers on art (who were also artists in their own right) to philosophical ideas of their age—ideas of which they were sympathetically aware, but which they had considered in none too philosophical a manner. And although Dolce, who does

48. Compare, for instance, Varchi's use of the word *discrezione* (see note 40) to suggest merely that the artist should alter and improve the raw material of nature with Lomazzo's very different and highly significant use of it in his last work, *Idea del tempio della pittura*, Milan, 1590, 12-14, where as a result of Neo-Platonic influences near the end of the sixteenth century, the term is used to mean that inner perceptive faculty of the artist which enables him to behold in his own mind the emanation of the supreme Idea of beauty which is in God, and to discern in this emanation the standard of perfect art. This theory of imitation differs fundamentally from the earlier theory of Dolce who finds an outward standard of perfection in the antique, not an inward standard in the image of ideal beauty in the mind's eye. The *locus classicus*, however, for Lomazzo's Neo-Platonism is chapter XXVI of the same book, entitled "Del modo di conoscere e constituire le proporzioni secondo la bellezza," in which, following Ficino's famous commentary on Plato's *Symposium*, he develops the theory that earthly beauty is an immaterial emanation of the divine beauty which the artist recognizes only because he is aware of the reflection of the divine beauty in his own mind (see Panofsky, *Idea*, pp. 52-56; for the reprinted texts of Ficino's commentary and Lomazzo's chapter *ibid.*, pp. 122-30; see note 108).

49. *L'idea del pittore, dello scultore e dell'architetto*, a lecture given before the Accademia di San Luca in Rome in 1664 and printed in 1672 as introduction to his *Vite de' pittori, scultori et architetti moderni*.

50. Alberti was aware of the concept of selective imita-

tion: he tells the famous story of Zeuxis; his statement that "the Idea of the beautiful escapes the inexperienced artist" (*Della pittura*, p. 151) is typical of an age that associated artistic achievement with experiment and practice. Raphael writes in 1516 to Castiglione that if he will paint a beautiful woman, it is necessary to see many beautiful women, but since there is a scarcity of handsome models, he makes use of a certain Idea that comes into his mind. This Idea or mental image of beautiful womanhood he probably associated with his experience of the individual beauty of women, but he cannot be said to have had in mind any very definite approximation of Aristotle's theory of the selective imitation of nature. The Idea may also have had some association in his mind with the Platonic idea of absolute beauty about which he could have heard much from Castiglione and others, but, again, writing as an intuitive artist, not as a humanist or philosopher, he does not say so. Vasari's remarks on the Idea (Introduction to the 1568 edition, pp. 168 ff.) have been explained by Panofsky to mean that it is derived empirically from experience of nature. But Vasari was no theorist and cannot be said to have given much thought to the classical doctrine of imitation. See the important discussion of the concept of the Idea during the Renaissance in Panofsky, *Idea*, pp. 23 ff. Panofsky cites and discusses all of the passages mentioned here. Friedlaender's Neo-Platonic interpretation of the passage in Vasari in his review of Panofsky's *Idea* (*Jahrbuch für Kunstwissenschaft*, VI, 1928, 61–62) in my opinion overemphasizes the importance of what rather appears to be a very slight adumbration of Neo-Platonic theory.

not use the term "Idea," clearly anticipates a theory that Bellori a century later was to clothe in more philosophical language, his remarks on imitation lack any really considered theoretical basis.[51] Bellori was then the first to combine the twin tendencies of the Italian mind into what, despite its own philosophical inconsistencies, may reasonably be called a theory of art.[52] Moreover, in proclaiming external nature to be the source of those ideal conceptions that are the objects of artistic imitation, he redirected the theory of painting, after its Platonic interlude during the age of Mannerism, into the Aristotelian tradition where it was to abide as long as classicism prevailed. And in so doing he once and for all validated Aristotle's *Poetics*, already enthroned in literary theory, as a capital document for the theory of painting as well.

Although the Neo-Platonic beginning of his treatise and the terminology throughout have led certain critics to consider him a "Platonist,"[53] Bellori's theory was in a fundamental sense, as Panofsky has demonstrated, opposed to that of the Neo-Platonic critics of the preceding century. For Bellori redefined the Idea that an artist should imitate, not in terms that a thoroughgoing Platonist would commend, but as an image of selected and embellished nature[54] which the painter forms in his imagination after the empirical method of Zeuxis who, being without benefit of the a priori presence of the Platonic Idea in his mind's eye, before he painted the ideal beauty of Helen fashioned for himself in a business-like way a composite mental image of the chief perfections of his five handsome models.[55]

51. See notes 40 and 43.

52. Cf. Panofsky, *op. cit.*, p. 61. He makes the point that Bellori's definite formulation of a theory that had already existed without such formulation in Renaissance criticism was the result of his opposition to Mannerism on the one hand, and on the other hand to the naturalism of Caravaggio who, says Bellori, like Demetrius (mentioned in Aristotle's *Poetics*), painted things as they are (not, the implication is, as they ought to be). Cf. note 12.

53. See Schlosser-Magnino, *La letteratura artistica*, p. 591: "Il ragionamento del Bellori è prettamente platonico." This is incorrect. There is plenty of adventitious Neo-Platonism in Bellori, but for a true Platonist the Idea would have unqualified, metaphysical existence independent of nature. Bellori's own opinion (*op. cit.*, p. 10) that it was Plato's meaning "che l'Idea sia una perfetta cognitione della cosa, cominciata su la natura" is only true if taken to mean that sense perception is the initial stimulus which prompts the mind to rise to a contemplation of that ideal truth or beauty of which the things of earth are only imperfect copies. For Plato, of course, the soul has knowledge of the ideas before birth, and sense perception merely serves to recall this knowledge. But in the very next sentence Bellori speaks of "Natura istessa, da cui deriva la vera Idea," which is a flat contradiction of the Platonic doctrine of a priori knowledge. Cf. Panofsky, *op. cit.*, p. 136, note 2.

54. See Panofsky's discussion of Bellori's theory (*ibid.*, pp. 57–63) to which I am greatly indebted. Panofsky has demonstrated the renewed interest in nature in Bellori's doctrine of ideal imitation and has noted that Bellori was the first to formulate what became among the French theorists of the age of classicism the doctrine of "la belle nature." The whole of Bellori's treatise on the Idea is reprinted in an appendix at the end of Panofsky's book.

55. Bellori, *op. cit.*, pp. 3–5 (unless otherwise noted, my discussion of Bellori's theory is based on this important passage):

"Quel sommo ed eterno intelletto autore della natura nel fabbricare l'opere sue maravigliose, altamente in se stesso riguardando, costituì le prime forme chiamate Idee, in modo che ciascuna specie espressa fù da quella prima Idea, formandosene il mirabile contesto delle cose create. . . . li

nobili Pittori e Scultori, quel primo fabbro imitando, si formano anch'essi nella mente un esempio di bellezza superiore, e in esso riguardando emendano la natura senza colpa di colore e di lineamento. Questa Idea, overo Dea della Pittura e della Scultura aperte le sacre cortine de gl' alti ingegni de i Dedali e de gli Apelli, si svela a noi e discende sopra i marmi e sopra le tele; originata dalla natura supera l'origine e fassi originale dell'arte, misurata dal compasso dell'intelletto diviene misura della mano, e animata dall'immaginativa dà vita all'immagine. Sono certamente per sentenza de' maggiori filosofi le cause esemplari ne gli animi de gli Artefici, le quali risiedono senza incertezza perpetuamente bellissime e perfettissime. Idea del Pittore e dello Scultore è quel perfetto, ed eccellente esempio della mente, alla cui immaginata forma imitando si rassomigliano le cose, che cadono sotto la vista: tale è la finitione di Cicerone nel libro dell'Oratore a Bruto. 'Ut igitur in formis et figuris est aliquid perfectum et excellens, cuius ad excogitatam speciem imitando referentur ea quae sub oculis ipsa cadunt, sic perfectae eloquentiae speciem animo videmus, effigiem auribus quaerimus.' Così l'Idea costituisce il perfetto della bellezza naturale, e unisce il vero al verisimile delle cose sottoposte all'occhio, sempre aspirando all'ottimo ed al maraviglioso, onde non solo emula, ma superiore fassi alla natura, palesandoci l'opere sue eleganti e compite, quali essa non è solita dimostrarci perfette in ogni parte. Questo pregio conferma Proclo nel Timeo, dicendo, se tu prenderai un huomo fatto dalla natura e un altro formato dall'arte statuaria, il naturale sarà meno prestante, perche l'arte opera più accuratamente. Me Zeusi, che con la scelta di cinque vergini formò l'immagine di Elena tanto famosa da Cicerone posta in esempio all'Oratore, insegna insieme al Pittore ed allo Scultore a contemplare l'Idea delle migliori forme naturali, con farne scelta da vari corpi, eleggendo le più eleganti.

"Imperochè non pensò egli di poter trovare in un corpo solo tutte quelle perfettioni, che cercava per la venustà di Helena, mentre la natura non fa perfetta cosa alcuna particolare in tutte le parti. 'Neque enim putavit omnia, quae quaereret ad venustatem, uno in corpore se reperire posse, ideo quod nihil simplici in genere omnibus ex partibus natura expolivit.' "

Aristotle had associated the nature and the excellence of artistic production with the knowledge of universals derived from particular experience,[56] and in a passage that hints at the idealizing function of art and anticipates the story of Zeuxis in later writers, he had remarked that the superiority of the painter's art over real objects lay in his having collected scattered excellences into one composite example of them all.[57] And when Bellori asserted that the Idea—the fair object of the painter's imitation—was derived from nature by a process of selecting the best, despite his use of Platonic terminology he was well aware, as were the French theorists of the age of classicism, that a similar concept underlay the theory of imitation in the *Poetics*. For the imitation of men better than ourselves, of life as it ought to be, in the pattern of an ideal tragedy, implies a highly discriminating selection of materials from the world of human character in action. It should be remembered, however, that at the beginning of his discourse Bellori in Platonic language that recalls the writing of his Mannerist predecessors had described the Idea as an "esempio de bellezza superiore" in the artist's mind, comparing it with the ideal pattern in the mind of God that had been the divine exemplar of the created world; and Bellori had further recalled the opinion of the greatest philosophers that the "cause esemplari,"[58] or ideal types after which works of art are fashioned, abide in the minds of artists (like the divine ideas in the heaven of Plato's *Phaedrus*) in the perfection of imperishable beauty. But while in his lofty preamble he is investing the Idea with this Platonic dignity, Bellori with a philosophical inconsistency of which he was certainly unaware[59] can simultaneously proclaim its origin in nature (*originata della natura*) and define it as the perfection of natural beauty (*il perfetto della bellezza naturale*). And during the remainder of his discourse[60] he leaves no doubt in the reader's mind that he thought of the Idea not primarily as an archetype of beauty existing a priori in metaphysical independence, but as derived a posteriori by a selective process from the artist's actual experience of nature. Furthermore, it is through the selected truth of art that the Idea manifests its superiority to the factual truth of nature from which, however, it takes its origin (*originata della natura, supera l'origine, e fassi originale dell'Arte*). Thus a renewed interest in nature as the source of ideal conceptions is central to Bellori's thought which reflects, at least to this extent, an empirico-idealistic, or generally Aristotelian, point of view as thoroughly characteristic of the Baroque seventeenth century as the mystical and Platonic point of view had been characteristic of the preceding period of Mannerism. And although he is still strongly aware of the absolute beauty of Plato that had haunted the imagination of the Renaissance—indeed he praises the Idea with the perfervid language of the Platonic enthusiast[61]—Bellori in giving the

---

56. *Metaphysics* I. I, 981a: "γίγνεται δὲ τέχνη ὅταν ἐκ πολλῶν τῆς ἐμπειρίας ἐννοημάτων μία καθόλου γένηται περὶ τῶν ὁμοίων ὑπόληψις." Aristotle goes on to say that experience is a knowledge of particulars, art of universals, and to suggest that the wisdom of artists resembles that of philosophers.

57. *Politics* III. 6, 1281b. Socrates had been reported by Xenophon to express a similar concept (*Memorabilia* III. 10, 1), and Plato, despite his hostility to painting, had remarked on its idealizing function when he compared his ideal state to a painter's picture of an ideally beautiful man, adding that the painter would not be any the less a good painter if he could not prove that it is possible for such a man to exist (*Republic* v. 472). These passages are cited by Panofsky (*op. cit.*, pp. 7–8). The story of Zeuxis is found in Cicero's *De inventione* (II. I, 1) where Bellori read it (he quotes from it at the end of the passage quoted in note 55). It had also been readily available to the Renaissance in Pliny (*Hist. nat.* xxxv).

58. For the *cause esemplari* see perhaps the passage in Plato's *Phaedo* (100c) in which it is argued that the absolute beauty is the cause (αἰτία) of beauty in all things that partake of it. But cf. Seneca *Epistolae* LXV. 2 ff. (quoted by Panofsky, p. 76). After defining the four Aristotelian causes, Seneca adds: "His quintam Plato adicit exemplar, quam ipse ideam vocat."

59. See Friedlaender (*op. cit.*, p. 63) for some interesting comments on Bellori's inconsistencies.

60. Cf. another such direct statement as: "Tutte le cose . . . dall'arte . . . hanno principio dalla Natura istessa, da cui deriva la vera Idea" (*op. cit.*, p. 10). See note 63.

61. Dryden at the beginning of his partial translation of Bellori's discourse which he included in his *Parallel between Painting and Poetry* (pp. v ff.) remarks that Bellori's *Idea of a Painter* "cannot be unpleasing, at least to such who are conversant in the Philosophy of Plato"; at the end he makes the following pregnant comment on Bellori's style: "In

theory of painting an Aristotelian orientation was the first writer in the seventeenth century to formulate what became the cardinal doctrine of French classicism—the doctrine of
"la belle nature."[62]

It is worth observing in this connection that Bellori's attitude towards the antique is
entirely reasonable, if one makes allowance for his century's excessive admiration of it. For
Bellori no more than Dolce considered the ancient statues objects of imitation in themselves,
but found them significant only as glorious examples of the work of artists whose claim to
the admiration of posterity is precisely that, selecting the best from nature, they imitated
the Idea of the beautiful. The example of the antique thus teaches the modern artist that
if he too will contemplate the fair Idea of that which he will represent—for the Idea of the
beautiful divides itself into various forms: "the brave, and magnanimous, and jocund,
and delicate of every age and of both sexes"—he will in some measure, at least, succeed
as antiquity succeeded.[63]

After Bellori, despite his residual Platonism, has effectively restated the theory of
imitation in Aristotelian fashion by re-affirming the source of the Idea in nature, he recalls
Aristotle's advice to the tragedians to follow the good painters in imitating life as it ought
to be, adding in a curious juxtaposition of the Aristotelian and the Platonic that "to make
men fairer than they commonly are and to choose the perfect belongs to Idea."[64] And then
in precise Aristotelian language he defines painting as the representation of human action.[65]
Thus he states what earlier critics hinted or took for granted, that painting like poetry is
an imitation of human action of more than common beauty or significance. And in this
connection one may recall the thoroughly humanistic and Aristotelian observation of Poussin, who more profoundly perhaps than any critic understood the significance of *ut pictura
poesis* for the painter's art, that without action drawing and color in painting are of no
avail.[66]

II—INVENTION

Poussin also gave expression to another aspect of the doctrine that obtained all through
the period of Renaissance and Baroque criticism, and like the theory of imitation to which
it was closely related, underwent a certain development. "The novelty in painting,"

---

these pompous Expressions, or such as these, the Italian
has given you his Idea of a Painter; and though I cannot
much commend the Style, I must needs say there is somewhat in the matter: Plato himself is accustom'd to write
loftily, imitating, as the Criticks tell us, the Manner of
Homer; but surely that inimitable Poet had not so much of
Smoak in his Writings, though not less of Fire. But in
short, this is the present genius of Italy."

62. See note 54. Cf. Babbitt, *The New Laokoön*, pp. 10–11.

63. *Op. cit.*, pp. 11 ff.: "Ci resterebbe il dire che gli antichi Scultori havendo usato l'Idea meravigliosa, come habbiamo accennato, sia però neccessario lo studio dell'antiche
sculture le più perfette, perche ci guidino alle bellezze
emendate della natura; . . . li Pittori e gli Scultori, sce-
gliendo le più eleganti bellezze naturali, perfettionano
l'Idea, l'opere loro vengono ad avanzarsi e restar superiori
alla natura, che è l'ultimo pregio di queste arti, come habbiamo provato. Quindi nasce l'ossequio e lo stupore de gli
huomini verso le statue e le immagini, quindi il premio e gli
honore degli Artefici; questa fù la gloria di Timante, di
Apelle, di Fidia, di Lisippo."

64. *Ibid.*, p. 8; he translates from *Poetics* xv: " . . .
insegna al tragico li costumi de' migliori, con l'esempio de
buoni Pittori, e Facitori d'immagini perfette, li quali usano
l'Idea: e sono queste le parole: 'Essendo la tragedia imita-

tione de' migliori, bisogna che noi imitiamo li buoni Pittori;
perchè quelli esprimendo la propria forma con farli simili,
più belli li fingono. ἀποδιδόντες τὴν οἰκείαν μορφὴν, ὁμοίους
ποιοῦντες, καλλίους γράφουσιν.'

"Il far però gli huomini più belli di quello che sono com-
munemente, e eleggere il perfetto, conviene all'Idea. Ma
non una di questa bellezza è l'Idea; varie sono le sue forme,
e forti, e magnanime, e gioconde, e delicate, di ogni età e
d'ogni sesso."

65. *Ibid.*, p. 9: " . . . essendo la Pittura rappresentatione
d'humana attione."

66. In Bellori, *Le vite dei pittori*, p. 461 (his collection of
Poussin's observations on painting appended to the *Vita*):
"Due sono gli strumenti, con che si dispongono gli animi
degli uditori: l'attione e la dittione, la prima per sè stessa
è tanto valevole ed efficace, che Demostene le diede il
principato sopra gli artifici rettorici, Marco Tullio perciò la
chiama favella del corpo, Quintiliano tanto vigore e forza
le attribuisce, che reputa inutili li concetti, le prove, gli
affetti sensa di essa, e sensa la quale inutili sono i lineamenti
e'l colore." This passage in which Poussin applies to
painting some ancient criticism of oratory is interesting as
an indication of the great influence which the ancient
rhetoricians exerted on Renaissance theorists in reinforcing
the Aristotelian view that painting is essentially an imitation of human life. Cf. note 97.

he said, "does not consist principally in a new subject, but in good and new disposition and expression, and thus the subject from being common and old becomes singular and new."[67] The conservative Horace who did not forbid but discouraged the creation of a new subject as an impractical venture, and who, as we have seen, found a standard of perfection in Greek literature of a bygone age, had advised the dramatic poet to adopt the safe and sane course of adhering to fables that tradition had made familiar;[68] and the later critics followed suit in their belief that invention (*inventio*), a term that regularly included the choice of subject as well as the general planning of the composition, should concern itself principally with traditional themes. From the time of Alberti it had been assumed, if not actually stated, that the only painter worthy of the name was the painter of history[69]—that is, of any fable ancient or modern, sacred or profane, that history or poetry, esteemed as liberal studies, might provide.[70] It was inevitable that the Bible and the ancient writers should supply most of these, and that in time scriptural and antique subject matter should be considered almost as indispensable to good invention as a knowledge of antique sculpture to good design.

Now this notion might be very well and even profound in the mind of a distinguished *peintre-philosophe* like Poussin, whose integrity of intellect, poetic insight, and subtlest inventiveness in composition could transform traditional material into an art of uniquely sophisticated originality. But in the mind of a shallow and uninventive painter of the academic type it might, like the dangerous counsel to imitate ancient art, easily lead to a corruption of Aristotle's theory of imitation; for it could encourage the imitation of famous paintings that had treated brilliantly the most important "histories," rather than of nature itself. And the study of nature, Poussin would have agreed, must always serve as the beginning even for the renewing of time-honored themes.

It was actually the French theorists of the seventeenth century who first declared the noble subject to be a *sine qua non* of the grand style that aimed at universal truth through the imitation of "la belle nature";[71] for the great events of scripture, or of Greek and Roman fable or history, "which," as Reynolds later observed, "early education and the universal course of reading have made familiar and interesting to all Europe without being degraded by the vulgarism of ordinary life in any country,"[72] easily adapted themselves to ideal representation. But the Italian critics of the sixteenth century had already implied this doctrine (it was better implied than formulated!) in urging the painter, as Quintilian had urged the orator, to acquire at least a competent knowledge of the poets and historians without which, all critics of art and literature were agreed, fine invention is impossible; and to cultivate the acquaintance of learned men.[73] A century before, the humanistic Alberti had

67. *Ibid.*, p. 462: "La novità nella Pittura non consiste principalmente nel soggetto non più veduto, ma nella buona, e nuova dispositione e espressione, e così il soggetto dall'essere commune, e vecchio diviene singolare, e nuovo." Cf. the very similar remark of Torquato Tasso regarding the novelty in epic poetry which Poussin may well have had in mind: "La novità del poema non consiste principalmente in questo, cioè che la materia sia finta, e non più udita; ma consiste nella novità del nodo e dello scioglimento della favola" (*Le prose diverse di T. Tasso*, ed. Guasti, Florence, 1875, I, 12).

68. *Ars poetica* 128–31:

"Difficile est proprie communia dicere; tuque rectius Iliacum carmen deducis in actus quam si proferres ignota indictaque primus. publica materies privati iuris erit."

Ibid., 268–69:

"vos exemplaria Graeca nocturna versate manu, versate diurna."

69. See Alberti, *Della pittura*, p. 105: "Grandissima opera del pictore sara l'istoria"; p. 109: "Grandissima opera del pictore con uno colosso! ma istoria, maggiore loda d'ingegnio rende l'istoria che qual sia colosso."

70. See Appendix 2, "*Inventio, Dispositio, Elocutio.*"

71. See note 78.

72. *Discourse* IV.

73. See Cicero, *De oratore* I. 34, 158: "Legendi etiam poetae, cognoscendae historiae, omnium bonarum artium doctores et scriptores eligendi et pervolutandi"; I. 16, 72, after he has noted the close affinities between orator and poet: "sic sentio neminem esse in oratorum numero habendum, qui non sit omnibus eis artibus, quae sunt libero

already reminded the painters that it was from Homer that Phidias in ancient times had learned to represent Zeus with divine majesty.[74] And for Lomazzo near the end of the sixteenth century the sentiment of history is the nurse of good composition producing gravity and truth; and painters are like poets not only in possessing "il furor d'Apolline," the divine inspiration of which Plato had spoken in the *Phaedrus*, but also in having as objects of representation the illustrious deeds and glory of heroes; for he cannot be a painter who has not also something of the spirit of a poet.[75] It is, moreover, always implied in the critical writing of this time that the painter, like Horace's poet,[76] should be a profound student of human nature which his knowledge of literature, in providing him with appropriate examples of human action and emotion, will also enrich. But whether it is a question of literary knowledge, or of immediate experience of life, for good painting as for good writing *sapere*, as Horace had said, *est principium et fons;* and that *eruditio libero digna*, that "learning worthy of a free man" of which Cicero had written,[77] is the inspiration equally of painters and of poets.

The French Academy inherited this humanistic point of view; and during the seventeenth century, at least, maintained the superiority of the historical painter over all others. After remarking that the mere representation of things in line and color is a mechanical process, and that you can tell a good painter by a difficult and noble invention, Félibien in an interesting passage arranges painters in hierarchical order according to the kind of subject matter which they prefer. The lowest type is the painter of still-life, and thence one proceeds through painters of landscape, of animals (a better subject than landscape, because animals are living and moving, not dead!), and of portraits to the *grand peintre*. He,

---

dignae, perpolitus." Quintilian, *Inst. orat.* x. 1, 27: "Plurimum dicit oratori conferre Theophrastus lectionem poetarum. . . . *Namque ab his in rebus spiritus et in verbis sublimitas et in adfectibus motus omnis et in personis decor petitur*"; cf. Dolce, *Dialogo*, pp. 170–72: "Et è impossibile, che il Pittore possegga bene le parti, che convengono alla inventione, si per conto della historia, come della convenevolezza, se non è pratico delle historie e delle favole de' Poeti. Onde si come è di grande utile a un letterato per le cose, che appartengono all'ufficio dello scrivere, il saper disegnare: così ancora sarebbe di molto beneficio alla profession del Pittore il saper lettere. Ma non essendo il Pittor letterato, sia almeno intendente, come io dico, delle historie, e delle Poesie, tenendo pratica di Poeti, e d'huomini dotti." But Dolce also argued (*ibid.*, p. 251) that poets could learn from painters: if Raphael's painting of Alexander and Roxana recalls Lucian's famous description (*Herodotus*, chap. 4–6), so Virgil owed his Laokoön to the Rhodian sculptors. With Dolce's remarks on the "pittor letterato," one should compare Daniello's advice to the poet to become learned if he would produce fine inventions (*La poetica*, Venice, 1536, p. 27). Armenini, *De'veri precetti della pittura*, III, 15, pp. 234–35, shows the pedantic preciseness and the moral and religious bias of the Mannerist critic in exhorting the painter to read the Bible, the lives of Christ, the Madonna, the sainted Virgins and Martyrs, the saints' legendary, the lives of the Church Fathers, etc. Among profane works he advises first Plutarch; then Livy, Oppian, etc., and "gli uomini illustri del Petrarca, le Donne illustri del Boccaccio, e per la favola la Geneologia degli Dei del medesimo; di Alberico, cioè del Cartari, le Trasformazioni di Ovidio, o come è d'Antonio Apulejo, e l'Amadigi di Gaula"; cf. Lomazzo, *Idea*, p. 36.

74. *Della pittura*, p. 147: "Fidias, più che le altri pictori famoso, confessava avere imparato da Homero poëta,

dipingiere Jove con molta divina maestà. *Cosi noi studios d'imparare più che di guadagnio, da i nostri poeti impareremo più et più cose utili alla pictura.*" Alberti may have owed the content of this passage to Valerius Maximus, *De factis dictisque memorabilibus*, III, 7. Janitschek (in his edition of Alberti, *op. cit.*, p. 244) finds a source in Strabo, *Geography*, VIII, C 354; cf. the tribute to Homer as the greatest creator of images of the gods that Dio Chrysostom puts into the mouth of Phidias (*Twelfth, or Olympic Discourse*, 57 ff.). Varchi, following Pliny, states (*Due lezzioni*, p. 116) that Zeuxis and Apelles owed respectively to Homer "le donne grandi e forzose," and "Diana fra un coro di Vergini"; he is archaeologically askew when he adds that the Campidoglio wolf was made after the image described by Cicero and later by Virgil.

75. Lomazzo, *Trattato*, VI, 2, pp. 281 ff.: ". . . il sentimento dell'istoria, che di qui ne nasce la buona compositione, parte tanto principale nella pittura che tanto ha del grave, e del buono, quanto è più simile al vero in tutte le parti . . . poeti, a' quali i pittori sono in molte parte simili; massime che cosi nel dipingere, come nel poetare vi corre il furor d'Apolline, e l'uno e l'altro ha per oggetto i fatti illustri, e le lodi de gl'Heroi da rappresentare . . . Anci pare per non so quale consequenza che non possa essere pittore, chi insieme anco non habbia qualche spirito di poesia"; Lomazzo may have remembered here the saying of the elder Philostratus (*Imagines* I. 294k) that poets and painters contribute equally to our knowledge of the deeds and appearance of heroes; Reynolds writing on the grand style (*Discourse* IV) associates historical painting with the poetical: "In conformity to custom, I call this part of the art historypainting; it ought to be called poetical, as in reality it is."

76. Cf. *Ars poetica* 309 ff.; especially 317–18:
"respicere exemplar vitae morumque iubebo
doctum imitatorem et vivas hinc ducere voces."

77. *De oratore* I. 5, 17.

imitating God whose most perfect work is also man, paints groups of human figures and chooses subjects from history and fable. "He must," writes Félibien, "like the historians, represent great events, or like the poets, subjects that will please; and mounting still higher, be skilled to conceal under the veil of fable the virtues of great men, and the most exalted mysteries."[78] Less than forty years later, at the beginning of the eighteenth century, this humanistic point of view had already begun to change and to point towards the still distant Romantic Movement, when the forward-looking critic Roger de Piles daringly extended the meaning of "historical invention" to include any choice of objects that "simply of themselves represent a subject for the painter."[79] It would have been in the interest of clarity had De Piles allowed the term to retain its original connotation of "having to do with fable," and invented a more appropriate category in which to place still-life and landscape painting. But if his new and inclusive use of it is not particularly apt, his desire to extend the welcome of criticism to those essentially pictorial provinces of the painter's art that the Academicians strenuously bred in the tradition of classicism—and of *ut pictura poesis*—had hitherto considered little more than hack-work, is historically very significant. At the end of the eighteenth century Reynolds, who combined allegiance to the grand style of historical painting with a breadth of outlook that recalls De Piles, said all that it is necessary to say in criticism of the academic hierarchy of the styles when he remarked: "Whether it is the human figure, an animal, or even inanimate objects, there is nothing, however unpromising in appearance, but may be raised into dignity, convey sentiment, and produce emotion, in the hands of a painter of genius. What was said of Virgil, that he threw even the dung about the ground with an air of dignity, may be applied to Titian: whatever he touched, however naturally mean, and habitually familiar, by a kind of magic he invested with grandeur and importance."[80] Reynolds' point would have greater force for the modern reader had he chosen Chardin rather than Titian as an illustration, although Chardin would certainly not have been so perfect a pendant to Virgil. But no liberal humanist of today will deny that individual genius is a more important factor than choice of subject matter in producing painting that is humanly significant, even though he will not admit—

---

78. See Félibien's preface to his *Conférences de l'Académie Royale de Peinture et de Sculpture*, Paris, 1669. The *Conférences* are reprinted in vol. v of the edition of his *Entretiens sur les vies et sur les ouvrages des plus excellens peintres* published at Trevoux in 1725; I quote from p. 310: "Il est constant qu'à mesure qu'ils [painters] s'occupent aux choses les plus difficiles et les plus nobles, ils sortent de ce qu'il y a de plus bas et de plus commun, et s'anoblissent par un travail plus illustre. Ainsi celui qui fait parfaitement des paisages est au-dessus d'un autre qui ne fait que des fruits, des fleurs, ou des coquilles. Celui qui peint des animaux vivans est plus estimable que ceux qui ne représentent que des choses mortes et sans mouvement; et comme la figure de l'homme est le plus parfait ouvrage de Dieu sur la terre, il est certain aussi que celui qui se rend l'imitateur de Dieu en peignant des figures humaines, est beaucoup plus excellent que tous les autres . . . un Peintre qui ne fait que des portraits, n'a pas encore atteint cette haute perfection de l'Art, et ne peut prétendre à l'honneur que reçoivent les plus sçavans. Il faut pour cela passer d'une seule figure à la représentation de plusieurs ensemble; il faut traiter l'histoire et la fable; il faut représenter de grandes actions comme les Historiens, ou des sujets agréables comme les Poëtes; et montant encore plus haut, il faut par des compositions allégoriques, sçavoir couvrir sous le voile de la fable les vertus des grands hommes, et les mystères les plus relevez. L'on appelle un grand Peintre celui qui s'acquitte bien de semblables entreprises." Félibien's remarks on allegory derive from the Renaissance theory of epic poetry, which was, of course, current in the seventeenth-century France. The epic was supposed to contain a hidden meaning beneath the veil of the action. See Spingarn, *op. cit.*, pp. 107.

79. De Piles is still conservative enough to remark that it is reasonable to consider a history (he means a history in Félibien's sense of the term) the highest kind of painting, and that it is usual to contrast a history with a painting of beasts, or of landscape, or of flowers, etc. Nevertheless, in including under the term "historical invention" (in contrast to what he calls allegorical, and mystical invention), true and fabulous history, portraiture, views of countries, beasts, and all the productions of art and nature, he is saying something new; and he shows a highly complimentary attitude toward the painter even of "the flower, fruit, plant, and insect" in remarking that even subjects such as these, that are not found in books or established by tradition, make demands on the painter's intelligence and inventive genius, and, he adds (and this is an old-fashioned compliment that no seventeenth-century Academician would have given any painting but a history in the strict sense of the word), are capable of yielding instruction. See *Cours de peinture*, pp. 53-55.

80. *Discourse* XI.

and neither, certainly, would Reynolds—that (granting them to be equal in purely pictorial skill) the painter of still-life is in the last analysis the equal of the painter of human action and emotion. For it is one thing to admit that in the minds of the Academicians *ut pictura poesis* was a doctrine that tended to circumscribe and formalize the art of painting, denying it conditions proper to its own development; it is another to deny with the aesthetic purists of the twentieth century that there is any virtue in the doctrine whatsoever.

In the mid-eighteenth century Lessing was in the curious position of objecting not only to *ut pictura poesis* as it was exemplified in the historical painters, but also to those critics of the doctrine who, like De Piles, approved an enlargement of the painter's legitimate sphere of activity. Looking backward like the theorists of the Italian Renaissance to the authority of Aristotle, and opposed to romantic tendencies in eighteenth-century criticism, he was, moreover, influenced by the rather narrow purism of Winckelmann's tendency to identify beauty with Greek statuary. Believing that bodily beauty is the end of painting ("the highest bodily beauty is, therefore," he says, "the highest end") he could only think of landscape painting and still-life, whether painted by an artist of genius or not, as inferior forms of art. But he had an even lower opinion, as he himself remarks, of historical painting wherein he thought that painters showed their cleverness in mere expression without subordinating the latter to bodily beauty. Lessing and Félibien would have argued violently concerning the scope and importance of historical painting; nevertheless it is possible that Lessing had the French critic in mind when he wrote a series of preparatory notes for the *Laokoön* in which, much like Félibien, he arranges painters in hierarchical order from those who paint landscape and still-life to those who paint mankind; the important difference being that for Félibien the highest ranking painter is the historical painter who paints significant human actions, whereas for Lessing he is the painter who subordinates everything to "körperliche Schönheit."[81]

These notes of Lessing epitomize the rigorous classicism of his attitude towards the figure arts, but they also indicate how little he understood the nature and possibilities of the art of painting. Apropos of his statement that "the highest bodily beauty exists only in man and even in him only by virtue of the ideal," a modern critic has made the following pertinent comment: "For Lessing, as for the classicist in general, beauty does not consist primarily in expression, but in a certain informing symmetry and proportion that, like true plot in tragedy, points the way to some human end."[82] This is undoubtedly true, and one will admire the fundamental humanist in Lessing and the objective clarity of his method of arguing from first principles. One will also admit that the stupid or blatant rhetoric of much academic art of the seventeenth and eighteenth centuries, and a disproportionate emphasis on expression among the critics, justified to a very great extent his dislike of historical painting wherein he saw bodily beauty, for him the chief *raison d'être* of painting, sacrificed to expression which might legitimately predominate in poetry but in

81. *Nachlass C.* (ed. Blümner, pp. 440–41):
"Der Ausdruck körperlicher Schönheit ist die Bestimmung der Mahlerey.

"Die höchste körperliche Schönheit also, ihre höchste Bestimmung.

"Die höchste körperliche Schönheit existiert nur in dem Menschen, und auch nur in diesem vermöge des Ideals.

"Dieses Ideal findet bey den Thieren schon weniger, in der vegetabilischen und leblosen Natur aber gar nicht Statt.

"Dieses ist es, was dem Blumen- und Landschaftsmahler seinen Rang anweiset.

"Er ahmet Schönheiten nach, die keines Ideals fähig sind; er arbeitet also bloss mit dem Auge und mit der Hand; und das Genie hat an seinem Werke wenig oder gar keinen Antheil.

"Doch ziehe ich noch immer den Landschaftsmahler demjenigen Historienmahler vor, der ohne seine Hauptabsicht auf die Schönheit zu richten, nur Klumpen Personen mahlt, um seine Geschicklichkeit in dem blossen Ausdrucke, und nicht in dem der Schönheit untergeordneten Ausdrucke, zu zeigen."

82. Babbitt, *The New Laokoön*, p. 46.

painting should remain strictly subordinate.[83] Yet it must be admitted that Félibien's definition of the greatest painting as that which represents serious actions, or delightful fables, or significant allegory—in short his allegiance to the doctrine *ut pictura poesis*—affords far wider and richer scope to the pictorial art than Lessing's austere and circumscribing definition. For although Lessing's avowed purpose in the *Laokoön* was to dispel a confusion between the temporal art of poetry and the spatial art of painting, in defining the end of painting as the representation of bodily beauty he unconsciously confused painting with sculpture. Seeking to destroy a confusion that originated in the Renaissance, he fell into another that originated in the antiquarian and archaeological research of the eighteenth century and was, in a sense, "hoist with his own petard."

Thus the fate of *ut pictura poesis* was various among critics of painting in the eighteenth century. De Piles and Reynolds, both of whom adhered to the spirit of the doctrine, could nevertheless implicitly criticize its exclusive character by welcoming within the painter's legitimate precincts matter that the French Academicians of an earlier day had considered profane. Lessing, far more conservative, would have agreed with Félibien that without subject matter drawn from human life, no painting is worthy of the name. But in his effort to purify the art of those elements that encouraged it, in the name of expression, to go beyond the limits of an art of figures coexistent in space, he tended to minimize the importance for the painter of human emotion and psychology. Instead, he adopted a narrow conception of formal beauty as the goal of painting—"beautiful shapes in graceful attitudes"; these alone, he remarked, among the "pictures" of Homer, the painters had found suitable to their proper powers. Had Lessing's conception of formal beauty been less restricted, critics of painting and aestheticians would be less inclined to quarrel with him, for no one will deny the general rightness of his contention that the greatest painting, like the greatest poetry, observes the limitations of its medium; or that it is dangerous for a spatial art like painting to attempt the progressive effects of a temporal art like poetry. Where Lessing went astray as a critic of painting was in defining its limits too strictly, and this appears nowhere more clearly than in his failure to take sufficiently into account that great middle-ground of human content on which both poetry and painting, as arts of expression, are equally free to draw. He was not unaware of this ground, but his reasonable objection to painting with literary intentions, his utter lack of understanding of the pictorial significance of the development of modern painting, and the dominant influence of the antique all combined to narrow his conception of formal beauty to a point that could allow the painter little room for the expression of human emotion.[84]

83. Lessing remarked (*Laokoön*, XVII) that the poet Kleist had he lived would have refashioned his descriptive poem *Frühling* in such a way as to convert "a series of pictures scantily interwoven with sentiments (*Empfindungen*) into a series of sentiments sparingly interspersed with images." For Lessing's objection to descriptive poetry as trespassing on the province of the painter's art, see note 29. He believed, of course, that progressive action (which would include "a series of sentiments") was the province of the poet.

84. Lessing's approbation of the expression of emotion in painting is characteristically confined in the *Laokoön* to certain ancient paintings, e.g., Timanthes' *Sacrifice of Iphigenia*, about which he had read in Pliny or elsewhere, but of which he could have had no direct experience. He has nothing to say in favor of expression in any modern painting. On the contrary, he objects (*Laokoön*, III) to that enlargement of the realm of art in modern times which has permitted it to extend its imitations over all of visible nature in which beauty has only a small share, and he objects to the fact that truth and expression, not beauty, have become the first law of art. He praises Zeuxis (*ibid.*, XXII) who, although he knew Homer's famous lines in which the elders express their admiration of Helen's beauty, limited himself to painting only her naked beauty, and he violently objects to the painting based on the same lines in Homer that the Comte de Caylus proposed for modern artists: Helen covered in a white veil on the walls of Troy in the midst of Priam and the elders—a painting in which the artist must exert his particular skill, says Caylus, to make us feel the triumph of beauty in the eager looks and expressions of astonishment on the faces of the elders. Lessing's excellent doctrine of the fruitful moment for the plastic artist (*ibid.*, III) in which he was to some extent anticipated by Shaftesbury, Du Bos, and Caylus himself, rightly limits the depiction of expression to that least transitory moment

Lessing's well-known objection to allegory offers further interesting comment on the puristic character of his attitude towards painting. Commenting in his preface to the *Laokoön* on the famous aphorism of Simonides,[85] he remarks with a large measure of truth that the modern fashion of allegorical pictures is the result of the mistaken effort on the part of painters to turn their art into mute poetry "without having considered to what extent painting can express universal ideas without giving up its proper métier and becoming an arbitrary method of writing" (*zu einer willkührlichen Schriftart zu werden*). In condemning allegory on the grounds of its arbitrary character, Lessing was anticipated by the Abbé du Bos, who though willing to admit that traditional allegorical figures have acquired the rights of solid citizenship in the arts, cannot tolerate their younger brethren that have issued from the fertile brains of modern painters. "Ils sont des chiffres," writes Du Bos, "dont personne n'a la clef, et même peu de gens la cherchent."[86] He goes on to say that the mingling of real and allegorical figures destroys verisimilitude (Aristotle's dramatic probability), and that Rubens' painting of the birth of Louis XIII, which he admits to be magnificent, would give more pleasure had the painter substituted for his allegorical personages women of that time who, in assisting Marie de'Medici during her travail, might have shown the various human emotions that such an event would cause. "Painters are poets," adds Du Bos, "but their poetry does not consist so much in inventing idle fancies (*chimères*) or 'jeux d'esprits,' as in conceiving what passions and what sentiments one should give to people according to their character and the condition of life in which one supposes them to be, just as it consists in discovering the expressions that will suitably render these passions apparent to the eye and enable one to perceive what these sentiments are."[87] Lessing would have agreed with Du Bos in detesting the obscurity of much allegorical painting—an obscurity that resulted from what, as we have seen, he called "an arbitrary manner of writing"; and although he does not develop the implications of this phrase, one may be certain that he means the idiosyncratic use of allegorical figures to serve as a kind of extended literary comment on the action in a painting. He would, however, have objected to the way in which Du Bos identifies the poetical element in painting with expression; for, as we have seen, Lessing considered expression far more appropriate to poetry than to painting, believing that in the latter it tended seriously to interfere with the all-important depiction of bodily beauty. Now no one will deny that the seventeenth and eighteenth centuries produced a host of obscure, vapid, and thoroughly tiresome allegories that would drive anyone at moments to espouse the "probability" of a Du Bos, or the purism of a Lessing. One may, in fact, go so far as to say that in allegory the art of painting, for reasons of which Du Bos may have been more aware than Lessing, has never achieved its most profound interpretation of human life. Nevertheless Lessing's downright objection to allegory is another clear indication of the one-sidedness of his criticism, and of his insensitiveness to the purely pictorial, as well as to certain imaginative, capacities of the painter's

in emotional experience which would permit the beholder of a picture to imagine in temporal terms more than the painter with his single moment of time could actually represent. But he never in the *Laokoön* comments on the application of this doctrine to expression in the work of any modern painter. He was evidently more interested in the kind of formal beauty that the unseen Helen of Zeuxis represented to him. For the "Menge schöner Körper, in schönen Stellungen" in Homer see *ibid.*, XVI. See p. 260 and note 305.

85. See p. 3 above.

86. *Réflexions critiques sur la poésie et sur la peinture*, 6th ed., Paris, 1755, I, 24, p. 194 (first ed. 1719). Cf. De Piles' earlier criticism of Le Brun on precisely these grounds (*Abrégé de la vie des peintres*, p. 511): Le Brun, he admits, treated allegorical subjects with much imagination, "mais au lieu d'en tirer les symboles de quelque source connue, comme de la Fable, et des Médailles antiques, il les a presque tous inventés, ainsi ces sortes de tableaux deviennent par-là des énigmes, que le spectateur ne veut pas se donner la peine d'éclaircir." Cf. note 176.

87. *Ibid.*, p. 197.

art. Of these Reynolds was fully aware when he wrote his opinion of the Marie de' Medici series; for although he agreed with Du Bos that Rubens was at fault in mixing allegorical figures with real personages, he also insisted that in sacrificing truth to nature, Rubens gained another kind of truth that was more significant. "If," says Reynolds, "the artist considered himself as engaged to furnish this gallery with a rich, various and splendid ornament, this could not be done, at least in an equal degree, without peopling the air and water with these allegorical figures; he therefore accomplished all that he purposed. In this case all lesser considerations, which tend to obstruct the great end of the work, must yield and give way."[88] Reynolds would have been the first to admit that painting can have a greater end than Rubens here fulfilled—such an end he discerned in the profound and overpowering invention of Michelangelo on the Sistine ceiling[89] the greatness of which, Reynolds knew, is no mere matter of rhetoric, or of pictorial brilliance, or, *pace* Lessing, of bodily beauty either; nevertheless, on the subject of pictorial allegory Reynolds spoke a more decisive word than Lessing when he continued his criticism of the Luxembourg paintings as follows: "It must always be remembered that the business of a great painter is to produce a great picture; he must therefore take special care not to be cajoled by specious arguments out of his materials.

"What has been so often said to the disadvantage of allegorical poetry,—that it is tedious, and uninteresting,—cannot with the same propriety be applied to painting, where the interest is of a different kind. If allegorical painting produces a greater variety of ideal beauty, a richer, a more various and delightful composition, and gives to the artist a greater opportunity of exhibiting his skill, all the interest he wishes for is accomplished; such a picture not only attracts, but fixes the attention."

Lessing would certainly have retorted that Rubens, like all painters of allegory, had been cajoled out of his main argument by specious materials. And in so saying, he would have again displayed that uncompromising dialectic that resulted in vital distinctions in his criticism of poetry and painting, but which, because he did not understand painting, and had adopted a narrow conception of her scope of imitation, left her, in reality, not a sister of poetry at all, but a kind of lesser sister of sculpture bereft of her proper sensuousness and of her proper range of expression. Lessing had excellent reasons both as a humanist and aesthetician for objecting probably to the bulk of allegorical painting. But he would not have been able to distinguish between the pictorial and imaginative brilliance of the Luxembourg series, and the "icily regular, splendidly null" allegorical histories, say, of Le Brun.

III—EXPRESSION

When Lessing objected to predominant expression in historical painting, he objected to something that the critics of the sixteenth century who developed the doctrine *ut pictura poesis* had insisted upon as fundamental. For if human beings in action are, as Aristotle said, the theme of painting, it follows that the movements of the body that express the affections and passions of the soul are the spirit and the life of art and the goal to which the whole science of painting tends. Lomazzo further insists that it is precisely here that painting most resembles poetry; for the inspired genius of both arts lies in the knowledge and power to express the passions, and the painter without expression, however perfect a stylist or technician he may be, must be prepared to endure the censure of posterity.[90] In the early Renaissance Alberti had included as essential to good composition an accurate

88. *Discourse* VII.
89. *Discourse* XV.

90. See Appendix 3, "Lomazzo on Expression."

knowledge of bodily movements as expressive of human emotion, citing Giotto's *Navicella* as a model for painters who would seek to be skilled in this most difficult and all-essential province of their art;[91] and throughout the whole critical tradition of classicism in Italy and France it is insisted not only that expressive movement is the life blood of all great painting, but that the painter himself, like Horace's tragic actor, if he is to move the beholder of his picture with the human emotions expressed therein, must first feel these emotions himself. *Si vis me flere, dolendum est primum ipsi tibi* is Horace's famous maxim[92] that served as a text for writers on expression in art and literature for more than two centuries.

This concern with the importance of expression in painting is not surprising among critics who believe that painting like poetry is an imitation of human life, and is, indeed, indispensable in any humanistic theory of the arts. For the humanist in insisting that great painting has the power through expressive movement to stir human emotion will readily agree with Horace that the artist must first possess in his own soul a capacity for deep and intense human experience. But the imaginative participation of the artist in the emotions of his characters is, to a greater or less extent, recreated in him who experiences a work of art; and it is when he speaks of this experience of the beholder that Lomazzo carries his theory of expression to an unfortunate extreme and shows the danger that dwells in any too emphatic insistence on the participation of the spectator in the emotions of persons represented in a picture. For surely all semblance of that essential detachment which in aesthetic experience mysteriously accompanies and qualifies emotional participation, is completely lost when Lomazzo, commenting on Horace's *si vis me flere*, observes that a painting in which the movement of the figures is rendered in life-like fashion (*con moti al naturale ritratti*) will cause the observer "to smile with him who smiles, think with him who thinks, . . . marvel with him who marvels, desire a beautiful young woman for his wife if he beholds a fair female nude in a picture, . . . desire to eat with him who eats precious and delicate foods, fall asleep with him who sweetly sleeps, etc."[93] This passage—an unconscious parody of Horace's remarks on expression, with painting assuming in a curious way the rôle of his tragic actor in its power to stir emotion in the spectator through the human emotions or sensations contained within its lines and colors (just as Horace's actor feeling grief would cause others to grieve)—is a kind of *reductio ad absurdum* as well of the modern theory of empathy. It is further interesting as showing the important influence that the typical Renaissance admiration of painting as a palpable and exact imitation of nature could have on a conscientious but confused critic who was attempting to deal with aesthetic ideas of a more advanced character. Lomazzo owes something here to Leonardo's praise of painting as superior to poetry in inciting men to acts of worship and of love through the realistic vividness of its imagery. That passage also contains the story of the man who always yawned when he beheld a certain figure yawning in a picture[94] and thereby recalls those stories of the efficacy of realistic art that delighted the writers of late antiquity[95]—stories more often extravagant than edifying that frequently recur in the

91. *Della pittura*, pp. 121 ff.

92. *Ars poetica* 102–3. Cf. Daniello, *La poetica*, p. 40: "Ne potrete voi ciò fare giamai se gli animi vostri non siano dentro commossi et infiammati prima"; Dolce, *Dialogo della pittura*, p. 226: "Ne puo muovere il Pittore, se prima nel far delle figure non sente nel suo animo quelle passioni, o diciamo affetti, che vuole imprimere in quello d'altrui. Onde dice il tante volte allegato Horatio, se vuoi ch'io pianga, è mestiero che tu avanti ti dolga teco."

93. Lomazzo, *op. cit.*, II, 1, p. 105.

94. *Trattato della pittura*, I, 25; cf. Cicero *De oratore* II. 44, on the power of the orator to rouse similar emotions.

95. Especially Pliny, *loc. cit.*; in the early eighteenth century the Abbé du Bos (*Réflexions critiques*, I, 38, p. 389), taking the part of the moderns sensibly observes that it would be foolish to give credence to the exaggerated accounts of the efficacy of ancient painting, and, because modern painting cannot achieve these same effects, judge that the latter is therefore inferior to the former.

critical writing of the sixteenth century. Thus when Armenini, remembering Plutarch, tells how Cassander trembled before the life-like portrait of the dead Alexander whom he had learned to fear, he illustrates with the authority of antique example the concept that painting as an art expressive of human emotion has power to move the beholder.[96] Horace, we have seen, was the foremost authority for this concept, but it should also be remarked that writers on expressive movement in painting, no less than critics of literature who were discussing the power of language to interpret and arouse the passions, also owed much to Cicero and Quintilian. For in shaping the education of the ideal orator, the ancient rhetoricians had been concerned not merely with words, but equally with gesture and facial expression as vital means of conveying human emotion. The Renaissance critics had, in fact, their invitation to compare painting with oratory in Quintilian's own observation that it is no wonder that gesture in oratory has a powerful effect on the mind, when the silent gestures in a painting can so penetrate to the heart that they seem to surpass in efficacy the power of speech itself.[97]

Alberti had counseled the painter to read the "*rhetorici*,"[98] and Leonardo may possibly remember Quintilian when he advises the painter to learn the fine points of expressive movement from the dumb whose only speech is gesture;[99] but virtually always, as one would expect, Leonardo based his remarks on expression not on written prescription, but on his own keen observation of human life. Thus when he compares the movements of arm and hand that accompany the words of the orator intent on persuading his audience with those movements which must, if the painter's illusion of life is to be convincing (all the more, in fact, because painting is mere illusion, not reality), unfailingly express the mental activity of the persons represented,[100] he is evidently not thinking of the counsel of a Quintilian, but remembering his own experience of advocates in the courts, including those stupid advocates who, as they sought to persuade without the proper use of gestures, resembled wooden statues—a warning to painters not to neglect the study of movement without which their own figures might seem equally wooden. Leonardo's conviction that painting which does not convincingly externalize the passions of the soul[101]—admiration, reverence, grief, suspicion, fear, joy, and the like—is, in his habitual phrase, "twice dead,"[102]

96. *Life of Alexander*, LXXIV; Armenini, *De' veri precetti della pittura*, I, 3, p. 30; cf. Alberti, *Della pittura*, p. 89.

97. *Inst. orat.* XI. 3, 67: "Nec mirum, si ista, quae tamen in aliquo posita sunt motu, tantum in animis valent, cum pictura, tacens opus et habitus semper eiusdem, sic in intimos penetret adfectus, ut ipsam vim dicendi nonnunquam superare videatur"; cf. XI. 3, 65 ff., and Cicero *De oratore* III. 59, a chapter on the significance of gesture and facial expression as indicative of the *motus animi* that follows one containing illustrations of these emotions from the poets. Cf. also Alberti, pp. 121–31; Dolce, pp. 108, 206; du Fresnoy, *De arte graphica*, 230 ff., and note how the latter declares it is the rhetorician's business to treat of the passions: "Hos ego Rhetoribus tractandos defero"; cf. note 66 for some relevant remarks of Poussin.

For the influence of the ancient theory of rhetoric on the Renaissance theory of poetry which, in regard to matters of expression, parallels its influence on the theory of painting, see Murray W. Bundy's introduction to Kelso's translation of Fracastoro's *Naugerius* (see note 31). The *Naugerius* is full of comparisons between the poet and the orator. Vida (*De arte poetica*, II. 496 ff.) advises the poet who seeks by the expression of human emotion to move his hearers to consult the eloquence of the great orators:

"Nec te oratores pigeat, artisque magistros

Consuluisse, Sinon Phrygios quo fallere possit
Arte, dolis quocunque animos impellere doctus;

* * * * *

Discitur hinc etenim sensus mentesque legentum
Flectere, diversosque animis motus dare, ut illis
Imperet arte potens, dictu mirabile, vates.
Nam semper, seu laeta canat, seu tristia moerens,
Affectas implet tacita dulcedine mentes."

98. *Op. cit.*, pp. 145–47.

99. *Trattato*, III, 376.

100. *Ibid.*, 368.

101. Leonardo succinctly states the dramatic theory of expression that was to become standard in all essentials throughout Renaissance and Baroque criticism of painting in the following passage (*ibid.*, 285): "et ancora ti ricordo . . . et sopra tuto, che li circonstanti al caso, per il quale è fatta la storia, sieno intenti à esso caso, con atti che mostrino *admiratione*, *riverentia*, *dolore*, *sospetto*, *paura*, *gaudio*, o' secondo che richiede il caso, per il quale è fatto il congionto o' uero concorso delle tue figure." Expression of the passions must, then, in each case be strictly related to the dramatic motive in the picture. This was to be the doctrine of the French Academy.

102. *Ibid.*, 297, 368, etc.

appears not only in his intense preoccupation as a draughtsman and painter with movement and facial expression, but also in the care with which he sometimes recorded in his writing the changing attitudes of the body under the stress of emotion, or the deformations of cheek, eyes, mouth, and hair.[103]

Nearly a century later Lomazzo's observations on expression lack entirely the empirical directness which was not to appear again in Renaissance or Baroque criticism. The product of a pedantic age, they are an elaborate prescription for the painter in which a few Leonardesque remarks on gesture and facial expression are scattered among a long array of examples of the passions in scripture, history, and myth, many of which must have been suggested to Lomazzo by their illustration in notable paintings of the Renaissance.[104] And frequently, following the ancient example of Cicero,[105] he quotes passages from the poets—chiefly Ariosto and Dante—which vividly portray human emotion, thereby giving substance to his earlier statement that it is in the expression of the passions that painting most resembles poetry.[106]

In his commentary first published in 1668 on Du Fresnoy's *De arte graphica*, Roger de Piles at the end of a disquisition on the passions in which one may detect his reading of the ancients, Alberti, Leonardo, and Lomazzo (such is the inevitable accumulation of critical pastiches as one moves forward in time), remarks with indubitable correctness that the latter has written at large in his second book on every passion in particular; but then has the good sense to deliver this warning to prospective painters: "Beware you dwell not too long upon it, and endeavor not to force your genius."[107] Here De Piles already gives evidence of a certain forward-looking distrust of the all-sufficiency of academic rules for the painter—a distrust which, despite his willingness to accept most of the doctrine founded on *ut pictura poesis* and his belief in the steadying effect of the rules, was to increase in his later writings; moreover, in his implication that genius should, in some measure at least, be free to spread its wings, he gives voice to an important doctrine that had already appeared chiefly under Neo-Platonic auspices in Italian criticism of the Mannerist age.[108]

---

103. See, for instance, the passage (*ibid.*, 385) in which, after remarking that the painter should vary the movements that occur with weeping and laughing according to the particular cause of these manifestations of emotion, Leonardo analyzes the bodily and facial movements that may accompany the former as follows: "Deli quai pianti alcuno si dimostra disperato, alcuno mediocre, alcuni solo lacrimosi, et alcuni gridano, alcuni col viso al cielo e co' le mani in basso, havendo le dita di quelle insieme tesute, altri timorosi, co'le spalli inalzate à gli orecchi; et così seguono secondo le predette cause. Quel, che versa'l pianto, alza le ciglia nelle loro giunture et le stringie in sieme, e compone grinze disopra in mezo li canti della bocca in basso; et colui che ride gli ha alti, et le ciglia aperte et spatiose." Cf. Appendix 5.

104. *Trattato*, II, *passim*. Cf. Appendix 5.

105. *De oratore* III. 58.

106. See note 90. Lomazzo frequently shows great discernment in choosing effective poetical illustration. How vivid, for instance, is the image of timid fear in the following lines from Ariosto's *Orlando furioso* (Canto I) where the poet is describing the flight of the beautiful Angelica through the forest from the amorous Rinaldo (*op. cit.*, II, 9, p. 128):

"E spesso il viso smorto adietro volta
Che le par che Rinaldo habbi alle spalle."

107. Dryden's translation, 2nd ed., London, 1716, p. 165.

108. The Neo-Platonic doctrine that beauty is essentially *gratia*—an emanation from the countenance of God

which is perceived by the artist in earthly things because he possesses and is aware of a like emanation in his own soul—gave a mystical character to the conception of beauty at the end of the Mannerist period that was opposed to the classical conception accepted by the Renaissance that beauty depends on proportion of parts. The association of the Idea of beauty in the artist's soul with a divine emanation means that the creative faculty, since it partakes of the absolute, can no more be forced into the groove of the rules than beauty can be defined in terms of mathematical proportion. See Lomazzo, *Idea*, chap. XXVI, and cf. the source material in Ficino, all reprinted in Panofsky, *Idea:* see note 48.—Cf. also the interesting passage in Zuccari, *L'Idea de' pittori, scultori ed architetti*, II, 6, p. 133 (quoted by Panofsky, p. 101) especially: "L'intelletto ha da essere non solo chiaro, ma libero, e l'ingegno sciolto, e non così ristretto in servitù meccanica di si fatte regole." Lomazzo (*Idea*, p. 8) remarks on the necessity of following one's own genius and of avoiding too close imitation of others. Genius should, however, be tempered with reason and study (*ibid.*, pp. 112 ff.). This was also the opinion of Du Fresnoy (30–36) who, well aware that "*normarum numero immani Geniumque moretur*," states that he is writing his *De arte graphica* in order to effect a reasonable compromise between genius and the rules. See the important discussion of the theory of art in the age of Mannerism in Panofsky, pp. 39 ff.; cf. *ibid.*, pp. 68 ff.

The notion that genius is inspired and that the "rules" are ineffective to produce great art goes back to a famous

And this doctrine in De Piles anticipates, four years before its translation by Boileau, the enormous influence that would gather momentum in the following century of the treatise of *Longinus on the Sublime*. De Piles was definitely influenced in his later writings by Longinus who had maintained that the sublime in art is the product of genius—of that inward greatness of soul that must from time to time inevitably transcend the rules, the correct observance of which by a lesser artist would result in mediocrity.[109]

Some thirty years later when the Longinian temper had grown upon him, De Piles again showed his skepticism of prescribed rules for expression when he criticized those definitions of the passions that Le Brun in his treatise on the subject had taken from Descartes' *Traité des passions de l'âme*. De Piles remarks truthfully and, one may hope, a little caustically, that these definitions are not always accommodated to the capacities of painters, who are not all philosophers, though in other respects they may not want sense and good natural parts.[110] He adds that Le Brun's definitions are very learned and fine but too general, and it is perfectly clear from the pages that follow that De Piles found the ancients who appealed to nature (he has Horace and Quintilian particularly in mind) more valuable sources of advice for the painters on this important subject than he found Le Brun, even though the latter's treatise carried with it the impressive sanction of the Cartesian philosophy. The modern reader of Le Brun's treatise will scarcely fail to agree with the opinion of De Piles, for nowhere did the aesthetic legislation of the Academy display itself in such absurdly detailed and absurdly abstract categories as in this attempt to specify the minute changes in facial expression by which each passion manifests itself through the complex action of those subtle vapors known as the *esprits animaux* which are the product of certain refinements of the circulatory system. One need not consider here the details of those deformations of pupil, eyebrow, nose, and mouth, or of those changes in complexion wrought by the *esprits* after sensory or imaginative stimuli have set them in motion. It should be remembered, however, that the treatise of Descartes, who shared the profound interest of his age in the *perturbationes animae*, was largely responsible for the special psycho-physiological character of the theory of expression during the last decades of the seventeenth century among the painter-theorists of the Academy who, legislating as they were for an art that would conserve the outward record of the soul's inner activity, were naturally far more precise in charting the details of expression than the philosopher himself had been. But behind the categorical exactitude with which they formulated the visible manifestations of these invisible states of the soul lay not only the rational thoroughness of the Cartesian method, but also the central concept of the Cartesian physics that the whole

---

passage in Plato's *Phaedrus* (245*a*): "But he who without the divine madness comes to the doors of the Muses, confident that he will be a good poet by art (ἐκ τέχνης), meets with no success, and the poetry of the same man vanishes into nothingness before that of the madman" (trans. H. N. Fowler, Loeb Classical Library, London and New York, 1928, p. 469). Junius (*De pictura veterum*, Amsterdam, 1637, I, 4, p. 22) applies the Platonic concept to painters as well as poets: "Utraque certe sequitur occulta quaedam naturae semina: unde persaepe videas cum Poetas, tum Pictores, ad amorem artis non tam provido multum diuque pensitatae rationis consilio duci, quam coeco quodam avidae mentis impetu trahi atque impelli." Lomazzo (see note 75) had already remarked that painters are like poets in sharing "il furor di Apolline." In insisting on the necessity of inspiration in artistic creation as opposed to reason (even though the latter also be encouraged to make its contribution), the Platonic tradition of the Renaissance prepared the way for the enthusiastic reception later of the doctrine of Longinus.

109. See note 311 and p. 68.

110. *Cours de peinture*, pp. 164 ff. It should be noted that after criticizing Le Brun, De Piles turns about and pays his respects to the famous Academician, remarking that his demonstrations may be of service to most painters. But certainly this is said without conviction and is merely a lukewarm and perfunctory salute to the tradition with which in this as in other respects, De Piles was often in disagreement. Descartes' treatise was published first in 1649. Le Brun's *Traité des passions*, as he called it in manuscript, was published first in Amsterdam and Paris in 1698 under the title *Conférence de M. Le Brun . . . sur l'expression générale et particulière*. The treatise is reprinted in Jouin, *Charles le Brun*, Paris, 1889, pp. 371–93.

universe and every individual body is a machine, and all movement, in consequence, mechanical.[111] Hence the exhaustively precise nature of Le Brun's anatomy of the passions which treats the body as a complex instrument that records with mechanical exactitude the invariable effects of emotional stimuli rather than as the vehicle of a humanly significant emotional life.[112]

Now no artist could undertake to follow precepts like Le Brun's without falling into the rut of arid formalism. It is enough for the artist, De Piles sensibly remarked, "without waiting for order or the judgment of reason" to know that the passions of the soul are caused by the sight of things and to ask himself how he would behave if seized with the passion that he would portray. But the rules for expression were nevertheless important to the honest theorists and second-rate painters of the Academy who with insufficient realization of the dangers that lurked about them, sought consciously to practice an exact, yet extensive pictorial rhetoric of gesture and facial expression that would both accord with their century's ideas of decorum and of "la belle nature" and satisfy its lively interest in the depiction of emotion. Through the heightened language of the drama, Corneille had created characters who embodied in typical mode the passions of the soul, and in the art of the greatest of French painters, whose profundity of mind and sentiment they never wholly understood, the Academicians discovered to their complacent satisfaction, and only with partial truth, a prefiguration of their chilling formulas for expression. Now everyone will acknowledge that the eminently rational genius of Poussin, who did not live to read the discourses of the Academicians, could invest the typical mode of rendering the passions with ideal signi̇ficance and grandeur, and no one will deny that his interest in the expression of the passions was the intensely scrutinizing interest of his age. But the writing of those who admired him as a master of expression—of Le Brun, Testelin, and others— might better, in part at least, be the writing of physiologists rather than of aestheticians, so analytically precise is the method by which they chart those visible changes in the face that accompany the "mouvements intérieures" within the body in experience of the emotions;[113] and although this type of quasi-scientific analysis could with its methodical prescriptions make a singularly barren contribution to the rules for good painting, it had nothing to contribute to the humanistic theory of the art. One may perhaps be permitted to quote at this point a remark of Addison's which, though it was made in another connection, is nevertheless appropriate here: "Great scholars are apt to fetch their comparisons and allusions from the sciences in which they are most conversant, so that many a man may see the compass of their learning in a treatise on the most indifferent subject. I have read a discourse upon love which none but a profound chymist could understand, and have heard many a sermon that should only have been preached before a congregation of Cartesians."[114] Certainly no Dolce, or Bellori, or even Lomazzo who at times yielded to few in the gentle art of multiplying profitless distinctions, would ever have remarked that it

---

111. See Appendix 4, "The Cartesian Theory of the Passions."

112. See Appendix 5, "Symposium on the Passion of Wrath."

113. The Cartesian psycho-physiological theory of expression that received its fullest statement among the Academicians in Le Brun's *Traité des passions* had first appeared in the *Conférences* of the Academy more than thirty years before the *Traité* was published in 1698, for instance in Van Opstal's discourse on the Laocoön in 1667, and to a less extent in Le Brun's discourse of the same year on Poussin's *Fall of the Manna* (Jouin, *Conférences de*

l'Académie, pp. 19–26; pp. 56–59). A fairly complete statement of the theory presented before the Academy in 1675 by Henri Testelin was published in 1680 in a collection of his discourses under the title *L'expression générale et particulière* (reprinted in Jouïn, *ibid.*, pp. 153–67). For further information on discussion of expression of the passions among the Academicians and for some excellent criticism of Le Brun's treatise see A. Fontaine, *Les doctrines d'art en France*, Paris, 1909, pp. 67 ff. See also the discussion of the influence of Descartes on the Academy in L. Hourticq, *De Poussin à Watteau*, Paris, 1921, pp. 42 ff.

114. *Spectator*, no. 421 (July 3, 1712).

was in the expression of the passions according to Le Brun that painting most resembles poetry.

It must be said, however, in favor of the Academicians that when they attempted during their *conférences* to analyze great masterpieces of painting, they habitually spoke of expression less in the psycho-physiological jargon of Descartes and Le Brun than in terms of the logical dramatic relationship of each figure in the painting to the cause of his emotion. Here, one should remember, another and far more significant aspect of the Cartesian philosophy exerted a dominant influence over the minds of the painter-theorists. This was the fundamental epistemological concept that the mind which knows itself more certainly than it knows the external world arrives at truth through the independently valid process of its own deductions, through its orderly procedure from one clearly-known proposition to another[115]—a concept that was reflected in the view of the critics that every element in a painting whether formal or expressive must as the logical part of a rational order unfailingly contribute to the demonstration of a central dramatic idea.[116] And this was a consummation which, theoretically at least, the painter could achieve only if the rules for historical invention, disposition or *ordonnance*, and coloring,[117] were scrupulously observed. "Dans cette même satisfaction d'une pensée bien conduite," writes a modern critic, "où Descartes avait discerné la vérité absolue, Le Brun plaça la beauté souveraine."[118] Félibien remarks that the expression of subsidiary figures in a painting is related to that of the protagonist as arms and legs to the human body,[119] and when he reports Le Brun's analysis of Poussin's painting of the *Fall of   e Manna in the Wilderness* (Fig. 1), he reports a discourse in which, it is true, some psycho-physiological commentary on expression is present, but in which the speaker is more particularly concerned with illustrating how diversely the characters in the pictorial drama react to the cause of their emotion; how diversely the expression of the passions is a dramatic illustration of the central idea of the painting—God's manifestation of his mercy to the suffering Israelites in causing the manna to descend upon them from heaven. "Monsieur Poussin," Le Brun is reported to have remarked in speaking of the expressions in the picture, "a rendu toutes ses figures si propres à son sujet, qu'il n'y en a

---

115. This concept is developed in "Méditation II" and in Part IV of the *Discours de la méthode*. In the latter occurs the famous *cogito, ergo sum*, the philosophical starting-point of the Cartesian logic and epistemology.

116. See Descartes' third precept of method (*Discours*, Part II): "De conduire par ordre mes pensées, en commençant par les objets les plus simples et les plus aisés à connaître, pour monter peu à peu comme par degrés jusques à la connoissance des plus composés, *et supposant même de l'ordre entre ceux qui ne se précèdent point naturellement les uns les autres....*

"Ces longues chaînes de raisons, toutes simples et faciles, dont les géomètres ont coutume de se servir pour parvenir à leurs plus difficiles démonstrations, m'avoient donné occasion de m'imaginer que toutes les choses qui peuvent tomber sous la connaissance des hommes s'entresuivent en même façon, *et que pourvu seulement qu'on s'abstienne d'en recevoir aucune pour vrai qui ne le soit, et qu'on garde toujours l'ordre qu'il faut pour les deduire les unes des autres*, il n'y en peut avoir de si éloignées auxquelles enfin on ne parvienne, ni de si cachées qu'on ne découvre." It is the certain knowledge of God that ultimately gives validity to the Cartesian method ("Méditation V").

With the passage above one may compare a passage in Félibien's preface to his *Conférences de l'Académie* (p. 307) in which he remarks that although in the observations of the *Conférences*, the absolute order of the "rules" for the

understanding of art is not preserved, nevertheless precepts are so often repeated apropos of the various pictures that are discussed, that "il ne laisse pas de s'en faire dans l'esprit un arrangement si juste [Félibien means an orderly conception of the rules], qu'en voyant un Tableau, toutes les notions que l'on a des parties qui peuvent servir à le rendre parfait, viennent sans confusion les unes après les autres, et en découvrent les beautez à mesure qu'on le regarde [these "parties" are later divided into those belonging to theory—as history (invention), decorum, expression etc.—and those belonging to practice—disposition, drawing, color etc.]. Ce qui arrivera de même à ceux qui voudront travailler après en avoir formé une idée, et bien conçû toute l'œconomie." One may say then, that just as the philosopher conducting his thoughts according to an order which is the abstract creation of the mind aims "by these long chains of reasons" at complex forms of truth, so the critic or the painter instructed in the rules will discover that his conceptions of those parts that are necessary to a perfect painting arrange themselves in his mind without confusion and in logical order; and that it is by virtue of these "chaînes des raisons" that the painter achieves that orderly pictorial truth that corresponds to the complex proposition of the philosopher.

117. See note 70. This is the old division of Dolce.

118. Hourticq, *op. cit.*, p. 59.

119. *Op. cit.*, p. 316.

pas une dont l'action[120] n'ait rapport à l'état où étoit alors le peuple Juif, qui au milieu du Desert se trouvoit dans une extrême nécessité, et dans une langueur épouvantable, mais qui dans ce moment se vit soulagé par le secours du Ciel."[121] Le Brun then proceeds to demonstrate how the dramatic event causes the expression of such varied emotions among the Israelites as admiration, joy, benevolence, fear, surprise, religious awe, and even feminine vanity of a sort, and he insists again that out of this diversity of psycho-physical reactions to the dramatic event Poussin has achieved pictorial unity not only because the different movements and facial expressions of the figures are always referred to the principal subject, but because the painter has selected his "expressions" in such a way that the picture has this further claim to impeccable logic of structure: like a drama on the stage, it observes the Aristotelian unity of action in having a beginning, a middle, and an end.[122] We shall discuss later this curious analogy between painting and dramatic poetry,—an analogy of more than doubtful validity yet a perfectly natural development of the doctrine *ut pictura poesis* under the impulse of the Cartesian passion for order and clarity.

Here we may note that Poussin himself evidently set great store by the diversity of emotional expression in this painting, for when after long labor to finish it, he finally despatched it to Chantelou, he wrote his friend that he would easily recognize those figures "qui languissent, qui admirent, celles qui ont pitié, qui font acte de charité, de grande necessité, de désir de se repaître, de consolation et autres, car les sept premières figures à main gauche vous diront tout ce qui est ici écrit et tout le reste est de la même étoffe." "Lisez l'histoire et le tableau," he adds, "afin de connaître si chaque chose est appropriée au sujet."[123] According to Poussin, then, the way in which to understand this painting is to "read" it, comparing it at the same time with the story in the twentieth chapter of Exodus. And although the critics would have looked carefully to see if the painter had been properly faithful to his text, Poussin does not advise Chantelou to "read" his picture merely that his friend may test his accuracy as an historical painter. This reading is rather to be a discriminating exercise of the intellect that will result in a judgment of the painting's excellence on more important grounds. A most fundamental condition of this excellence is the painter's ability to represent human emotions that are clearly appropriate to the sub-

---

120. By the general term action Le Brun means any movement of the body, including facial movement, that expresses inward emotion. See his explanation of "action" in Appendix 4.

121. Jouin, *Conférences*, pp. 55–56. The notion that expression must be strictly related to the central dramatic event—rendered "secondo che richiede il caso"—had been clearly stated by Leonardo (see note 101). And Lomazzo in selecting the Crucifixion as typical of a scene of human sorrow for which he is attempting to prescribe a good composition (*Trattato*, VI, 34, p. 363), tells how the grief in the painting, motivated by the dead figure on the cross, must vary according to the closeness of the relationship of the different figures to Christ. The figures will be arranged in the picture to form a kind of emotional crescendo as one moves from those at the greatest distance from the cross whose grief is the least, if it exists at all, to the overwhelming grief of John, and even more of Mary, at the foot of the cross in the center. The Academicians take over and develop the psychological implications of Leonardo's doctrine. For them "expressions" are not only "what the event requires"—not only have this strict dramatic relationship to the event—but are also external signs of a variety of emotions, typical of the male or female sex at various ages or in different conditions of life, which the

dramatic event as a kind of efficient cause has stimulated into activity. For the Academicians, then, with their interest in the passions of the soul, the "expressions" in Poussin's *Fall of the Manna* (Fig. 1) are not only dramatically related to the event by a direct causal connection (as the emotions in Leonardo's *Last Supper*, for instance, are related to the dramatic pronouncement of Christ) but each expression has also, as Le Brun says, its "cause particulière"—in the character or condition, that is, of the different persons represented. Poussin's painting is thus not only a pictorial drama, but within the dramatic frame of reference, it is also an analysis of the passions. The same might be said of Leonardo's *Last Supper* or his *Adoration of the Magi*, but in Leonardo the dramatic intensity and concentration are greater—the central composition forces one to view the passions almost entirely as rendered "secondo che richiede il caso"; whereas frequently in Poussin, the dramatic structure is looser, and the analysis of the passions appears to have something of its own excuse for being.

122. Jouin, *Conférences*, p. 64.

123. Letter of April 28, 1639. I quote from the modernized text in the edition of Pierre du Colombier, Paris, 1929, p. 12. For the original text see *Correspondance de Nicolas Poussin*, ed. Ch. Jouanny, Paris, 1911, p. 21.

ject—that are, Poussin means, representative of the behavior of different types of human beings under particular dramatic conditions.[124] And in insisting on the logic with which Poussin relates his complex human material to the dominant dramatic idea of his painting, Félibien and Le Brun show themselves, as we have seen, loyal disciples of the Cartesian doctrine that the reason has the power to impose its own valid order on "toutes les choses qui peuvent tomber sous la connaissance des hommes." Thus when the critics commented on the diverse, yet ordered rendering of the emotions in a painting, it was this doctrine which by and large intervened to discipline, if not actually dispel, the application of those elaborate rules for expression, gathered together by Le Brun, that reflected the mechanistic aspect of the Cartesian philosophy.

Something closely akin to the Cartesian rationalism was strong in Poussin himself who, like Descartes, distrusted the mirage of sense perception[125] and valued only that selected and ordered knowledge which it was alone within the power of the clarifying reason to attain. "Mon naturel," he wrote to Chantelou in a famous letter of 1642, "me contraint de chercher et aimer les choses bien ordonnées, fuyant la confusion qui m'est contraire et ennemie, comme est la lumière des obscures ténèbres."[126] This passage written by a man who may never actually have read Descartes to express his sense of confusion at being requested to do within a given time a great deal more than he knew he could do well, might nevertheless have been written in another connection by Descartes himself.[127] Some thirty years later when the admirable Boileau was writing in his *L'art poétique* what was to be perhaps the most influential statement in the history of French classicism of the rules for good poetry, he admonished the poets to love reason which alone could bestow value and lustre upon their labors,[128] and in a passage of which both the thought and the imagery remind one of Poussin's confession to Chantelou, remarks that only clear conceptions born of the light-dispensing reason, well thought out—in Poussin's phrase, "bien ordonnées"— could result in clarity and precision of literary form:

> Il est certains Esprits, dont les sombres pensées
> Sont d'un nuage épais toûjours embarrassées.
> Le jour de la raison ne le sçauroit percer.
> Selon que nostre idée est plus ou moins obscure,
> L'expression la suit, ou moins nette, ou plus pure.
> Ce que l'on conçoit bien s'énonce clairement.
> Et les mots pour le dire arrivent aisément.[129]

When Boileau summed up the rules which the Académie Française regarded as essential for correct writing in the various literary genres, he had been anticipated by a few years by those who legislated for the sister art of painting. Du Fresnoy's *De arte graphica*, based pretty squarely on Dolce and other Italians, owed the Cartesian philosophy little if anything. The author remarks, in fact, that he would not "stifle the Genius, by a jumbled

---

124. When Poussin tells Chantelou to read his picture in order to see if "each thing is suited to the subject," he may well have meant to include other things (setting, drapery, etc.), besides the expressions. But the latter were evidently of paramount importance. In fact in an earlier letter to the painter Jacques Stella he had already emphasized those "attitudes naturelles" which made manifest the joy, lightness of heart, admiration, respect, and reverence of the Jews on the occasion of the Fall of the Manna (Félibien, *Entretiens* no. 8, IV, 26).

125. For Descartes on the senses see "Méditations" I and VI.

126. Letter of April 7, 1642; quoted from Du Colombier,

op. cit., pp. 71–72 (Jouanny, p. 134). See the fine essay of Paul Desjardins on Poussin in *La méthode des classiques français*, Paris, 1904, pp. 165–233, to which Professor Friedlaender has called my attention.

127. Cf. Descartes at the end of Part I of the *Discours de la méthode:* "Et j'avois toujours un extrême désir d'apprendre à distinguer le vrai d'avec le faux, pour voir clair en mes actions et marcher avec assurance en cette vie."

128. *L'art poétique*, 1674, I, 37–38:

"Aimez donc la Raison. Que toujours vos écrits
Empruntent d'elle seule et leur lustre et leur prix."

129. *Ibid.*, 147–53.

Heap of Rules: nor extinguish the Fire of a Vein which is lively and abundant."[130] But
Félibien's preface to his report of six *conférences* of the Academy is, in its way, as complete
a summary of the rules for painting as is Boileau's *L'art poétique* of the rules for poetry;
and he is in perfect accord with Boileau's Cartesian dictum that clear writing attends upon
the clear conception of what one will write about, when he remarks that if an artist would
make a wise disposition in his mind of a work that he would execute, he must first "avoir
une connaissance parfaite de la chose qu'on veut representer, de quelles parties elle doit
être composée, et de quelle sorte l'on y doit procéder." And one could find no more thoroughly Cartesian definition of art than in the words which follow: "Et cette connaissance
que l'on acquiert, et dont l'on fait des règles, est à mon avis ce que l'on peut nommer
l'Art."[131] A perfect painting, then, like a perfect poem, is a logical construction of the
human reason, an architectonic *pensée* with every least part causally related to the informing dramatic purpose of the whole. And within the abstract perfection of this edifice of
the reason abide those rules which the mind may discover by the rational process of deduc-
tion—rules for invention, disposition, decorum, verisimilitude, expression, and the like—
the whole Draconian code of the French Academy. To the question: In what art do you
find that perfectly pure and cloudless *connaissance* from which you derive these rules?
—Félibien, like Boileau would, of course, have answered: The antique; and as one legislating also for the art of painting, would have added Raphael, and, of course, Poussin. To
the question: How binding are these excellent rules, and if you counsel the painter to observe
them faithfully, in what does the originality of painting consist?—he might have answered,
remembering Poussin, that within the precincts of the rules an intelligent and disciplined
genius will always achieve "good and new disposition and expression." The eighteenth
century was gradually to find this answer unsatisfactory, and in the end when the romantic
imagination had outlawed the rational art of an earlier day, when nature no longer signified
selected beauty or universal truth, and when genius had rejected forever the guiding hand
of the rules, it would be repudiated altogether.

But since it is less the purpose of this essay to discuss the dissolution of the doctrine
ut pictura poesis than to define its components and to sketch their development, it will be
well to return to the central track of the argument and to consider some other elements of
the doctrine that had their origin in the literary criticism of the ancients before they were
incorporated by the Italians into their humanistic theory of painting and became, at
length, essential elements of the aesthetic dogma of the French Academy. In the discussion that follows it will be further Horatian modifications of the Aristotelian theory of
imitation that will engage our attention. Horace's encouragement of invention based on
traditional forms and subjects, and his contribution to the doctrine of expression, have
already been discussed.

IV—INSTRUCTION AND DELIGHT

Directly adapted from Horace who as a satirist had held up the mirror of his art to
human foibles, and had a serious, if urbane and detached, concern for the improvement of
human life, came the admonition that painting like poetry (Horace had been thinking of
the effect of dramatic art on the audience) should instruct as well as delight.[132] This half-

---

130. Dryden's translation of ll.32–33. Du Fresnoy
may well be thinking of the compendious "regole" of
Lomazzo.

131. Pp. 307–8; cf. note 116.

132. *Ars poetica* 333 ff.:

"Aut prodesse volunt aut delectare poetae
aut simul et iucunda et idonea dicere vitae.
                        * * * * *
omne tulit punctum qui miscuit utile dulci,
lectorem delectando pariterque monendo."

moralistic definition of the purpose of art might not be consistent with the Aristotelian position that art as ideal imitation is founded on its own principles of structure and has no conscious didactic intent; but it was accepted axiomatically, if uncritically, by most Renaissance and Baroque critics both of poetry and painting,[133] for the excellent reason that it provided an ethical sanction, fortunately in the words of an ancient critic, for those arts which, if the subject matter were profane, the Middle Ages had accepted only with the aid of allegorical or moral interpretation, and which the divine Plato had excoriated, in a way frequently embarrassing to the Renaissance, as feeding and watering the passions.[134] And in modern Italy, almost within the memory of those mid-sixteenth-century critics who were shaping the new theories of painting and of poetry, Savonarola with the energy and conviction of a St. Bernard had denounced the arts as hostile to the Christian way of life.[135]

Poussin had written Fréart de Chambray that the end of art is delectation,[136] but in this case the Academicians preferred the opinion of Horace and of those Italian critics both of

133. Castelvetro among the critics of literature was early a distinguished opponent of the Horatian definition of the function of poetry, and he was correct in believing that those who held "that poetry aims at teaching or at teaching and delighting together" ran counter to the authority of Aristotle. See H. B. Charlton, *Castelvetro's Theory of Poetry*, Manchester, 1913, pp. 66 ff.

134. *Republic* x. In his *Genealogia deorum gentilium*, XIV, 19 Boccaccio refuses to believe that Plato really intended to banish from his ideal state poets of the caliber of Homer, Ennius, and Virgil "who withal was so pure that he blushed in mind as well as in countenance when he overheard an indecent remark among his coevals or others, and thus won the nickname Partheinas, that is, 'virgin,' or more correctly, 'virginity'" (trans. C. G. Osgood, Princeton, 1930, p. 91). In XIV, 9, occurs his Horatian definition of the purpose of poetry, and the notion that the ancient poets were men of wisdom whose works are full of profit as well as pleasure to the reader informs the whole work. In XIV, 6, occurs an interesting reference to the figure arts when Boccaccio, indignant at those who condemn poetry as futile and empty because there occur poems that sing the adulteries of the gods, asks "if Praxiteles or Phidias, both experts in their art, should choose for a statue the immodest subject of Priapus on his way to Iole by night, instead of Diana glorified in her chastity; or if Apelles, or our own Giotto—whom Apelles in his time did not excel—should represent Venus in the embrace of Mars instead of the enthroned Jove dispensing laws unto the gods, shall we therefore condemn these arts? Downright stupidity, I should call it!" (*ibid.*, p. 38). If occasional lapses are, therefore, no reason for condemning sculpture and painting whose business, Boccaccio would imply, is to improve mankind, no more certainly are they reason for condemning poetry which "offers us so many incitements to virtue." In thus implying a comparison between the figure arts and poetry on the ground that the function of both is to instruct as well as delight, Boccaccio pays an unusual, if indirect, compliment to the former as liberal arts some fifty years before Alberti wrote his *apologia* for painting in 1436. For Plato's criticism of the arts and the Renaissance justification of poetry, see Spingarn, *Literary Criticism in the Renaissance*, pp. 16 ff. I do not know any critic of painting who feels it necessary to defend painting against Plato's moralistic criticism of the arts, but objection occurs to his famous metaphysical argument in *Republic* x, that art is thrice removed from the truth, in a passage in Comanini's *Il Figino*, Mantua, 1591 (quoted by Panofsky, *op. cit.*, p. 97): Plato, it is affirmed, degrades painting and poetry when he declares that their works are imitations not of truth, but of "apparenti imagini" [things of this world that are only copies of the world of ideas; only shadowy images,

that is, of the truth]. The whole effort of Renaissance criticism was obviously to prove the contrary—that painting, like poetry, is an imitation of ideal truth, though not generally of the "ideas" in the a priori sense in which Plato conceived them. See Chapter II.

135. The idea that art should instruct mankind is found from the beginning in Renaissance criticism and is present in European criticism until the end of the eighteenth century. It is found in the observation of Alberti (*op. cit.*, p. 89) that painting is conducive to piety; Leonardo (*op. cit.*, I, 21) states that it can show "molti morali costumi," as in the *Calumny of Apelles;* Dolce (p. 208) does not mention instruction when he states that the poet's business is to delight, but his remarks on decorum (see notes 145, 159) are sufficient evidence that he was imbued with the Horatian maxim. At the end of the sixteenth century the critics reflect the spirit of the Counter-Reformation: Armenini (*op. cit.*, I, 3, pp. 38–40) writes of painting as furthering the cause of the Christian religion with its images, and Lomazzo (*Trattato*, VI, I, p. 280) speaks of the greatest paintings as "non per altro dipinte che per mostrar di continuo per gl'occhi a gl'animi la vera strada che si ha da tenere per ben vivere, e passar questi nostri infelici giorni fatti di chiaro, e scuro, con timore, et amor di quel Signore, la cui bontà volse formarci a sembianza de la divinissima imagine sua." That painting should both delight and instruct was standard doctrine of the French Academy: see Félibien, preface to the *Conférences*, p. 317; Antoine Coypel, *L'excellence de la peinture*, 1721 (Jouin, *op. cit.*, p. 217). The notion was still strong in Diderot, for instance in his approval of Greuze's sentimental, sham morality (Salon of 1767). Early in the eighteenth century, writers on aesthetics began to drop the didactic conception of art and to attempt an explanation in psychological and emotional terms of the pleasure which it is the function of art to afford. So Addison in his series of essays in the *Spectator* on the "Pleasures of the Imagination" (June 21 to July 3, 1712) which are an important document for the study of *ut pictura poesis* from the point of view of literature. See also the theory of Du Bos (*Réflexions critiques*, I, I ff.) that the pleasure of art, which is most intense when the subject is painful or terrible, is a necessary relief from the boredom of human life. This theory had wide influence in the eighteenth century, e.g. on Burke and Hume in England. At the end of the century Sir Joshua Reynolds, at once the disciple and frank critic of the academic tradition, abandoned the didactic theory. "The end of the arts," he says, "is to make an impression on the imagination and the feelings"; and the ultimate test of the arts is whether they answer "the end of art, which is, to produce a pleasing effect upon the mind" (*Discourse* XIII).

136. Letter of March 1, 1665 (Jouanny, p. 462).

poetry and painting who found in the arts an incitement to virtuous conduct and even, as Lomazzo had maintained, a guide in this vale of tears to righteous living in the Christian faith.[137] Now the ideal representation of human life as Aristotle conceived it does not make the artist in any sense a conscious moralist; nevertheless the spectacle in a great tragedy of one of high station and of superior human capacities brought to inevitable ruin, yet made wise through suffering that is out of all proportion to his fault, and maintaining his moral dignity even in the extremes of fortune, results, no one can deny, in an elevation and purification of the spirit, in that "calm of mind, all passion spent" of which Milton, remembering the Aristotelian catharsis, wrote at the close of *Samson Agonistes*. And the Academicians, for whom the highest achievement in painting lay in the incorporation of the καλὸς κ'ἀγαθός of the antique within the dramatic delineation of a noble subject that would, in a Christian or a Stoic sense, proclaim the dignity of man, were profoundly conscious that the rules were the vessels of moral instruction, and that painting like poetry should as Horace and Boileau enjoined:

> Partout joigne au plaisant le solide et l'utile.

And they would have added that the wise beholder of a painting like Boileau's "lecteur sage":

> fuit un vain amusement
> Et veut mettre à profit son divertissement.[138]

The didactic theory of art had among the writers and critics of literature an important corollary. When Sir Philip Sidney gave a moral interpretation to Aristotle's famous dictum that poetry is more philosophical than history by declaring that poetry is a popular philosophy, teaching by example rather than by precept,[139] he had behind him not only the influential opinion of Horace but also, it must be remembered, the medieval view expressed by Dante[140] and others that poetry is a guide and teacher of men. And at closer range he had been anticipated in the mid-sixteenth century by the Italian critic Fracastoro who had written that if the poet "imitates those things which pertain to the will, since they can produce wisdom and other virtues, surely the usefulness of this imitation and representation is incomparable. For those examples which we see in life make us much more wise and experienced than precepts."[141] A half century after Sidney, Milton writing in the same vein was to pay the highest tribute of all to what the critics believed to be the didactic power of the arts, when he declared that the poet Edmund Spenser, in his graphic description of the dangers of lust in the bower of the enchantress Acrasia,[142] had proved himself a better teacher than Scotus or Aquinas.[143] No one had ever paid the art of painting so lofty and perhaps so doubtful a compliment, though since the time of Alberti the beneficial effects of painting on mankind had been pretty assiduously catalogued.

V— DECORUM

Finally from Horace and closely related to his definition of the purpose of poetry came those ideas of decorum that fill many a dreary page of sixteenth- and seventeenth-century criticism and were, at least in part, responsible for the artificial and formulated expression of a Le Brun. And it may be useful at this point to sum up Horace's preponderant influence with the critics by remarking what the reader may have already observed—that it had the

137. See note 135.
138. *L'art poétique*, IV, 88–90.
139. *Defense of Poesy*, 1595, ed. Cook, Boston, 1890, p. 15.
140. See *ibid.*, p. XXXIII for citations from the *Vita*

Nuova, the letter to Can Grande della Scala, etc.
141. *Naugerius*, trans. Kelso, p. 68.
142. *Faerie Queene*, II, canto 12.
143. *Areopagitica*, 1644.

general result, on the whole unfortunate, of directing the Aristotelian theory of imitation into channels of formalism or didacticism. In the case of decorum (*convenevolezza* or *decoro*), a word to conjure with in the history of criticism, the painter was admonished that in his art each age, each sex, each type of human being must display its representative character, and he must be scrupulous in giving the appropriate physique, gesture, bearing, and facial expression to each of his figures. Horace had given similar advice to the dramatic poet,[144] and this advice the Renaissance critics of poetry elaborately included in their own *Ars poetica* which they based upon the criticism of antiquity.[145] Like so much in the doctrine *ut pictura poesis*, the classical concept of decorum found its first expression among the critics of painting in Alberti, when for instance he remarks that the movement of figures in a painting must be appropriate to their various ages, or that the hands of Helen of Troy or of Iphigenia must not be withered and rough[146]—an example of indecorum at which the modern reader will be inclined to smile, but which may have seemed to Alberti, in an age

144. See especially *Ars poetica* 153–78, which Horace sums up in the concluding lines:

"ne forte seniles
mandentur iuveni partes pueroque viriles,
semper in adiunctis aevoque morabimur aptis."

Besides warning against this kind of inappropriateness, Horace also advised both poet and painter to avoid deviations from nature represented by the monstrous or fantastic (see note 14), and the poet to avoid the unnaturally violent, e.g. Medea butchering her children on the stage (*op. cit.*, 182–88). Chiefly these passages from Horace and several from the rhetoricians, e.g. Quintilian *Inst. Orat.* XI. 3., 61 ff., were the sources for discussions of decorum from the fifteenth to the eighteenth century.

145. Daniello (*La poetica*, pp. 35 ff.) remarks that there must be decorum in the whole of a poem, which must not mix the serious and the light, that which is easy to understand with that which is profound, etc. One must not, in short, make a poem like one of the hybrid grotesques mentioned by Horace (see note 14). The following passage defines decorum very completely in terms of the appropriate and fitting: "Ne è solamente da vedere che le parti delle materie che si prendono a trattare, habbiano fra loro convenientia: ma che quelle anchora che alle persone si mandano, convenientissime, proprie, et accomodate siano. Et oltre accio, che il parlar che si da loro, sia di soavità, di mansuetudine, di gravità, d'allegrezza, di dolore, et finalmente pieno de gli affetti tutti, secondo però la qualità, la degnità, l'habito, l'ufficio, et l'età di ciascuna ... Et perchè questa convenevolezza non è altro che un cotal habito et proprietà dell'animo, è necessario che devendosi essa a ciascuna persona attribuire, si sappi somigliantemente et si conosca la consuetudine, et i costumi di ciascuna età." There follows a passage based squarely on the *Ars poetica* (153 ff.) about giving age and youth their appropriate characters; another to the effect that if one introduces "persone note," one must make them act as in previous authors (cf. *ibid.* 119 ff.); and a warning to the dramatic poet to avoid the cruel, impossible, and dishonest, in which Horace's example of Medea is mentioned.

Dolce published a translation of the *Ars poetica* in 1535, and his *Dialogo della pittura* of 1557 is, like Daniello's *Poetica*, steeped in Horace. On p. 162 Dolce quotes Horace (see note 14) on the fantastic creations that both poet and painter should avoid, and in another passage (pp. 152 ff.) in which he discusses *convenevolezza* he remembers several passages in the *Ars poetica* and probably Daniello (pp. 34–35) when, after remarking that Christ, and St. Paul preaching, are not to be rendered naked or clothed in a mean habit, and that the painter must have strict regard

"alla qualità delle persone, ne meno alle nationi, a costumi, a luoghi, et a tempi" observes that the same kind of decorum should obtain in poetry, referring to Horace's remark (119–27) that the poet must adapt the language of the speaker to the character he would represent, as with Achilles, Orestes, Medea, etc. The notion of decorum is very strong in Lomazzo, for whom each type of place (cemetery, church, royal palace, garden, musical instruments (!) etc.) and of subject (compositions of war, rape, love, banquets, joy, sadness, etc.) has its appropriate iconography. The greater part of Book VI of the *Trattato* is devoted to decorum.

146. The notion of decorum is nearly as dominant in the second book of Alberti's *Della pittura* as in Horace's *Ars poetica*. Alberti explains at length (pp. 111 ff.) that in the art of painting each part of the body must conform in its proportions to the other parts, e.g. a big head and a small breast do not go together; each member must act in a way that is suitable to what it is supposed to perform, e.g. it is appropriate for a runner to move the hands not less than the feet, and if a body is dead or alive, every least part must appear dead or alive; each part must likewise be appropriate to the type of person represented, e.g. Helen and Iphigenia must not have hands that are "vecchizze et gottiche," nor Ganymede a wrinkled brow, nor the legs of a porter; finally each part must conform in color to the other parts, e.g. a lovely face of fair complexion does not match a breast and limbs that are ugly and dirty-colored. And just as each part of the body must conform to the others in size, function, type, and color, so each figure in a composition must have the proper size as compared with the others and act in a suitable manner: e.g. at a brawl of centaurs, it would be silly if one of them should lie asleep overcome with wine in the midst of such tumult, and it would be wrong to put a man in a house the size of a jewel case where he could scarcely sit down ("which I often see," says Alberti, having in mind a habit of Trecento and early Quattrocento painters). The passage on the movements appropriate to virgins and to boys, mature men, and old men (pp. 127 ff.) reads like an adaptation of Horace's advice to the poet concerning the appropriate portrayal of the different ages of man (*op. cit.*, 153 ff.): "Et conviensi alla pictura essere movimenti soavi et grati, convenienti ad quello ivi si facci. Siano alla vergini movimenti et posari ariosi, pieni de semplicità, in quali piu tosto sia dolcezza di quiete che galliardia; ... Siano i movimenti ai garzonetti leggieri, jocondi, con una certa demostratione di grande animo et buone forze. Sia nell'huomo movimenti con piu fermezza ornati, con belli posari et artificiosi. Sia ad i vecchi loro movimenti et posari stracchi, non so,o in su due piè, ma ancora si sostenghino su le mani."

that had but lately awakened to the ideal beauty of the antique, as shocking an example as he could imagine. It is somewhat surprising to discover that at the end of the fifteenth century Leonardo counsels the painter to observe decorum in a passage that more than most in the *Trattato* savors of traditional theory. For one does not easily associate the implications of propriety and formalism that the term suggests with Leonardo's eager interest in the infinite variety of nature. Decorum he defines as "appropriateness of gesture, dress, and locality" and urges the painter to have due regard for the dignity or lowliness of things, for instance in the depiction of a scene at court wherein the beard, mien, and habit of the king must have a becoming dignity, and a like appropriateness must appear among the courtiers and bystanders according to the loftiness or humbleness of their position; and he ends by maintaining, like Horace and Alberti, that gesture in painting must be appropriate to age, and also, he adds, to sex.[147] Now if remarks like these which were to become standard for later criticism could be construed simply as advice to the painter to follow in the path of the typical and representative, avoiding the improbable and adventitious, no one could take exception to them. Yet despite their implications of the typical, they could not be so interpreted, because the very notion of decorum is allied less to the Aristotelian doctrine of typical imitation than to that pseudo-Aristotelian theory, already discussed, of the imitation of models.[148] The advice to imitate the antique was, as we have seen, fraught with danger to the creative artist, because the imitation of models, however perfect they might be, was not the fresh imitation of nature. And the concept of decorum, for similar reasons, was not one to encourage artistic originality. For when the critics told the painters to observe decorum, they were not actually advising them to follow the typical in human action and expression (which, if the artist's work is to be alive must be fashioned after the living face of nature). Rather, they were enjoining them to follow the typical formalized, reduced to static and convenient patterns that a person of good taste and good sense (he need possess no great imagination) would accept as appropriate symbols for the actions and emotions of people of such and such an age, sex, profession, situation in life, or whatever it might be.[149] And if one had asked the Italian and French critics where those appropriate formulas for typical representation had been embodied in sculpture and painting, they would have answered that decorum, like ideal beauty, had been a particular virtue of the antique, and in modern times of Raphael; and, the French Academy would have added, of Poussin.[150] Thus the classical notion of the typical or representative is preserved in the concept of decorum, but in a conventionalized form, just as the concept of ideal

147. *Trattato*, III. 377: "Osserva il decoro, cioè della convenientia del atto, vestiggie, e sito, e circonspetti della degnità o'viltà delle cose, che tu voi figurare, cioè, ch'il Re sia di barba, aria et abito grave, et il sito ornato, e li circonstanti stieno con riverentia e admiratione, e abiti degni et convenienti alla gravità d'una corte Reale. Et li vili disornati, infinti et abbietti. Et li lor circonstanti habbian similitudine, con atti vili et prosuntuosi, et tutte le membra corispondino à tal componimento, et che li atti d'un vecchio non sieno simili à quelli del giovane, nè la femina con l'atto del maschio, nè quello del huomo con quello del fanciullo."

148. See Chapter II and note 43.

149. It should be noted that in Horace's concept of decorum the implications of the typical are strong, so strong in fact that it may seem at times (as in 153–78 where he gives advice to the poet concerning the portrayal of youth, manhood, and old age) that the concept of the typical is scarcely to be distinguished from that of the appropriate (cf. also 317–18, wherein Horace urges the poet to go

directly to life for his materials—advice that would tend to counteract the formalistic implications of decorum); and it stands to reason that an artist who would represent the different ages of man in a fitting manner, must be aware of typical aspects of human life. Nevertheless, it is the notion of the appropriate that prevails in Horace, and the fact that he is conscious both of models in the art of the past and of the kind of thing his audience expects ("Tu quid ego et populus mecum desideret audi") is also characteristic of a mind that tends to think in terms of the conventional and becoming in art rather than of the profoundly imaginative and original. This would also be true of most Renaissance critics. See the remarks of Daniello and Dolce in note 145.

150. See Dolce, *Dialogo della pittura*, p. 160. Félibien in his reports of the fourth and sixth *Conférences* of the Academy records praise of Raphael's and of Poussin's decorum (Jouin, *Conférences de l'Académie*, p. 36 and p. 60). See note 183.

nature was preserved in the antique where it could always be found in convenient and invariable patterns.

There was another aspect of decorum not so specifically defined by Horace as were its connotations of the typical, but nevertheless present in the *Ars poetica*, and closely related to that inobtrusive tone of urbane admonition that informs much of the poem and changes to positive utterance near the end when the poet declares the didactic and moral uses of poetry,[151] and describes the noble rôle that the art has played in bringing civilization to mankind.[152] This was the notion, of great importance in the later history of criticism, that decorum means not only the suitable representation of typical aspects of human life, but also specific conformity to what is decent and proper in taste, and even more in morality and religion.[153] Although in this last sense it had been implicit in Alberti,[154] it is absent in the empirical Leonardo, for whom prescribed forms in morality and religion probably had little significance; but the examples of indecorum noted by the critics after 1550, and particularly towards the end of the century, nearly always suggest the immoral, irreverent, or undignified, rather than the unrepresentative or improbable; and the critics, mindful of what they consider the didactic function of art, are chiefly concerned that it shall be as edifying as possible. When Dolce in 1557 cites as reasonable and sound criticism Ghiberti's complaint to Donatello that when he made a crucifix he hung a peasant, not an ideal figure upon the cross,[155] or when he objects to Dürer's painting the Virgin and saints in German habits,[156] he speaks, one may believe, both as a man of classical taste who favored the generalizing, not the realistic, mode of representation, and as an apologist for propriety in religious painting. When Borghini, however, in 1584 blames Bronzino for the introduction of nudes into his *Christ in Limbo*,[157] he is no longer an aesthetic critic at all, but merely a moralist who sees in the irreverent treatment of the subject an incitement to carnal desire. But the most celebrated example of impropriety for the later sixteenth century was Michelangelo's *Last Judgment*, and the age of the Counter-Reform nowhere expresses itself in criticism more directly than in those writers who in the name of Horatian decorum take the heroic artist to task, not only for the mild aesthetic and factual impropriety of failing to distinguish between the sexes in the rendering of muscles, but especially for the very

151. See note 132.

152. *Ars poetica*, 391 ff.

153. Medea's butchering her children, and Atreus' cooking human flesh on the stage are shocking to Horace as well as a tax on his credulity (*ibid.*, 185–88). Part of that wisdom which is the source of good writing consists in learning what is fitting in the sense of moral obligation: if the poet has learned what he owes his country and his friends, what love is due a parent, a brother and a guest, as well as the professional duties of a judge or a general, he knows, Horace says, how to render his characters appropriately (*ibid.*, 309 ff.). In this passage decorum means what is decent and becoming in conduct as well as what is appropriate to typical conditions of human life. In 153 ff. it has the latter significance.

154. He remarks (*op. cit.*, p. 119) that in representing the nude, or naked parts, the painter must have regard for decency and modesty: "Et se cosi ivi sia licito, sievi alcuno ignudo et alcuni parte nudi et parte vestiti, ma sempre si serva alla vergogna et alla pudicitia." He adds that ugly parts of the body or those that have little grace must be covered with drapery, leaves, or the hand, and then characteristically cites the antique example of Antigonus whom the ancients represented in profile lest one should see the blemish of his blind eye; and other antique examples of the same kind. Cf. note 40.

155. *Op. cit.*, p. 154.

156. *Ibid.*, p. 156.

157. Raffaello Borghini, *Il riposo*, Florence, 1730 (first ed., Florence, 1584), p. 84: "Di già abbiamo noi ragionato... quanto mal fatto sia, le figure sacre fare così lascive. Ora di più vi dico, che non solamente nelle chiese, ma in ogni altro pubblico luogo discovengono; perciocchè danno cattivo esempio, e nella mente vani pensieri inducono: e gli artifici, che l'hanno fatte, nella vecchiezza dal tardo pentimento della coscienza sentono rodersi il cuore, come ben confessa Bartolommeo Ammanati scultore, in una sua lettera stampata, agli Accademici del Disegno, dove dice, aver malamente adoperato nell'aver fatto molte statue ignude.... Perciò quanta poca laude meriti il Bronzino in cotesta opera, voi medesimo, dilettandovi nel rimirare quelle donne lascive, il confessate: ed io son sicuro, che ciascuno, che si ferma attento a rimirare questa pittura, considerando la morbidezza delle membra, e la vaghezza del viso di quelle giovani donne, non possa fare di non sentire qualche stimolo della carne: cosa tutta al contrario di quello, che nel santo tempio di Dio far si doverebbe." The Counter-Reform here speaks very clearly, as it does in Lomazzo's injunction that lascivious subjects are permissible only "in modo che nulla di lascivo si veda, ma si cuopra con destrezza, e gratia" (*op. cit.*, VI, 2, p. 284).

serious violation of modesty, decency, and sacred truth in turning a sublime religious subject into a display of anatomical invention. Already in 1557 Dolce, speaking through the mouth of Aretino who some ten years before in his brilliantly abusive letter had told Michelangelo that his art belonged in a brothel rather than in the Sistine,[158] declares that in the chapel of God's earthly representative the nakedness of sacred personages is intolerable, and that improper pictures, far more than improper books—a curious extension, if one likes, of the implications of *ut pictura poesis*—should be placed upon the Index.[159] This severity of judgment, while it echoes the ironic hyperbole of the irreligious Aretino, is yet entirely in keeping with the spirit of the age, although Dolce who admired the rich naturalism of Titian and considered the classicizing Raphael the paragon of decorum, really objects to Michelangelo more, one may believe, on the grounds of style than of propriety, finding the Florentine's muscularity and violent action greatly to his distaste. In the next decade, however, a less humanistic critic, the cleric Gilio da Fabriano, who writes a dialogue on painting that is in good part an actual commentary on various passages from the *Ars poetica*,[160] just as if Horace had written the poem in the first place for painters rather than for poets, identifies decorum not only with a sense of reverent propriety due the mysteries of the faith, but also with the strict observance of the truth of scriptural narrative.[161] He blames Michelangelo[162] not only for the gratuitous nakedness of his figures,[163] or because the angels who bear the Instruments of the Passion comport themselves like acrobats,[164] but also because the wind appears to move hair and garments when there could have been no wind, "for on that day the winds and tempests will have ceased";[165] or the Resurrection occurs gradually with people now skeletons, now half now fully clothed with flesh, when St. Paul had written that it would be accomplished in the twinkling of an eye;[166] or people rise

158. For Aretino's letter see G. Gaye, *Carteggio inedito d'artisti*, Florence, 1840, II, 332–35.

159. *Op. cit.*, p. 236.

160. *Due dialoghi di M. Giovanni Andrea Gilio da Fabriano. Nel primo si ragiona de le parti Morali et civili appartenenti a Letterati, Cortigiani . . . nel secondo si ragiona degli errori de' Pittori circa l'historie con molte annotatione fatte sopra il Giuditio di Michelangelo*, Camerino, 1564. For discussion of Gilio see E. Steinmann, *Die Sixtinische Kapella*, Munich, 1905, II, 554–58; J. Schlosser-Magnino, *La letteratura artistica*, pp. 370–72.

161. Gilio also urges the painter throughout to observe decorum in the more general sense of what is appropriate to the different ages, sexes, countries, etc., quoting Horace as his authority: If the painter has due regard for this precept, he will not fall into what is indecent or unbecoming in his treatment of religious subjects. See, for instance, *ibid.*, p. 89: "Prima deve avvertire à dar le parti tanto sostantiali, quanto accidentali che se li [the persons to be painted] convengono, acciò si conservi il decoro in tutte le cose, tanto de l'età, quanto del sesso, de la dignità, de la patria, de'costumi, de gli habiti, de gesti, e d'ogn'altra cosa propria a l'huomo, del che diceva Horatio [*Ars poetica* 156–57]:

Tu dei notar d'ogni etade i costumi
E dare a gli anni mobili, ò maturi;
Et à le lor nature il suo decoro."

162. As a kind of introduction to his criticism of the *Last Judgment*, Gilio (pp. 83–84) notes other examples of historical error on the part of painters: e.g. it is wrong to represent St. Peter "decrepito," because from the time of the Crucifixion to the last year of Nero's reign when he was crucified, thirty-seven years had passed: nor should Joseph be so represented, because it is improbable (*non verisimile*) that God would have wished the Mother of His Son to be wedded to an aged man who could not endure

the hardship of the flight into Egypt, etc.; nor should the Magdalen, no longer a sinner, be represented clean, perfumed, and covered with jewelry, at the foot of the cross; nor is it fitting to show St. Jerome in the habit of a cardinal when it was not until seven hundred years later that Pope Innocent IV gave cardinals this habit; and furthermore, if St. Jerome was a hermit, it is wrong to represent him in worldly pomp, for these glorious saints deliberately chose a solitary life in order to make the flesh obedient to the spirit. All such comments are extremely interesting as illustrating the spirit of the Counter-Reform.

163. *Ibid.*, p. 105: Gilio remarks that it is no scandal to behold the nakedness of innocent children, but that if to behold the nakedness of men and women causes shame, how much more shameful is it to behold the nakedness of saints: ". . . però io dico, che se quelle parti consideriamo in piccioli fanciulletti, non ci scandalezziamo, havendo riguardo, à l'innocenza e purità di quelli, sensa malitia, e peccato: non potendoci per naturale istinto cadere. Ma se la miriamo ne gli huomini, e ne le donne n'arreca vergogna, è scandolo, e piu quando le veggiamo in persone, ed in luoghi ove vedere non si doverebbe: perche ne santi, oltra l'erubescenza, ne da non so che di rimorso ne l'animo, considerando, che quel santo non solo, ad altri mostre non l'harebbe: ma ne anche esso stesso miratele."

164. *Ibid.*, p. 90: "Per questo [because an artist should represent his subject truthfully and appropriately] io non lodo gli sforzi che fanno gli Angeli nel giuditio di Michelagnolo, dico di quelli che sostengono la croce, la colonna, e gli altri sacrati misteri; i quali piu tosto rappresentano mattaccini, ò giocolieri, che Angeli: conciosia che l'Angelo sosterrebbe senza fatica tutto'l globo de la terra: non che una Croce, ò una colonna, ò simili."

165. *Ibid.*, p. 93.

166. *Ibid.*, pp. 97–98; there is a long argument on this point in which Job, Ezekiel, and Horace are cited as well as St. Paul.

from the dead now decrepit and bald, now young, in fact of every age, when it is written
that on the last day there shall be no age nor youth, nor any deformity of body;[167] or the
Virgin turns away from Christ, as if fearing that she herself were unprotected from his
wrath;[168] or Charon's bark appears without the sanction of historical truth even though
Michelangelo owed its introduction to the greatest of Italian poets.[169] For poetry and
theology, says Gilio, are sharply opposed, and when Michelangelo painted an important
article of the faith, it was his business to imitate the theologians, not the poets.[170]

Gilio had, however, no objection to the poets provided the painter chose the proper
moment to use them. And in the categorizing manner of his age he divides painters into
three groups—poetical, historical, and mixed painters.[171] The first are like the poets in being
free to invent their subjects provided they follow Horace's advice to follow nature and avoid
the incongruous, whereas the second group, as we have seen, are not free to invent at all,[172]
at least if one includes in a definition of invention any imaginative treatment of one's religious or historical subject. The third group, who have much in common, says Gilio, with
the great epic poets of antiquity, mix fact with fiction in a delightful manner as Virgil did,
for instance, when he added the purely fabulous account of Aeneas' sojourn with Dido to
a story which in the main was historically correct.[173] And it is in the domain of allegory and
symbolism where fact and fancy frequently mingle that the painters owe much to the
antique poets, and even more to those sculptors who carved on the Roman triumphal arches
personifications of Victory, Peace, and the City of Rome, whence the Christians learned to
give human form to the theological virtues.[174] These are admitted in sacred art, Gilio
characteristically adds, "for no other reason than because they are virtues, for the purity
of religion wants nothing but what is virtuous, especially when it comes to allegorical
figures."[175] There follows a warning to the painters that recalls the later sentiments of
De Piles and Du Bos that the spectator must be able to understand these mixtures of truth
and fiction without undue mental effort.[176] And it is worth noting that Gilio's threefold
division of poetical, historical, and mixed painters has its later counterpart in the threefold
activity already discussed which Félibien was to assign to the *grand peintre* of the seventeenth century.

167. *Ibid.*, p. 107: "L'altro capriccio è [by *capriccio*
Gilio means Michelangelo's "caprice," his unwarranted
freedom of imagination which results in the violation of
sacred truth], che in quel giorno non ci sara ne vecchiezza,
ne pueritia, ne calvitie, ne cosa alcuna che renda il corpo
in qual si voglia parte difforme, come dianzi vi
dissi: e quivi si veggono decrepiti, calvi, fanciulli, e gente
d'ogni etade."

168. *Ibid.*, p. 107. It is argued that on the last day, far
from fulfilling her role of intercessor for humanity, she will
condemn with her son. But Michelangelo is finally allowed to be in the realm of "fintioni concesse" when he
renders the Virgin as she turns away from Christ, only
because he thereby shows the ignorant that she is (when
not assisting at the Last Judgment) the Mother of Mercy.

169. *Ibid.*, p. 108. Gilio fears that the ignorant will believe in the reality of poetic inventions: "L'altra cosa che
mi dispiace è che in uno articolo di tanta importanza
Michelangelo haggia framessa la favola di Caronte, che
con la sua alata barca passa l'anime de'dannati, per la
Stigia Palude; alzando il remo per batter quelle che
tardano ad entrare dentro, acciò dieno luogo a l'altre.
Pensate voi che gli ignoranti non credano fermamente,
che laggiù vi sieno fiumi, paludi, navi, giudici che rivedano
i processi, el Cane da tre Teste che riscuote la gabella?"

170. *Ibid.*, p. 109: "Però Michelagnolo dovendo
dipingere uno articolo de la nostra fede importantissimo
doveva imitare i Teologi, e non i Poeti, che la Teologia, e

la poesia si sono de diretto contrarie."

171. *Ibid.*, p. 75: "Perche doverebbono sapere, che il
pittore a le volte è puro historico, à le volte puro poeta, ed
à le volte è misto. Quando è puro poeta, penso che lecito
gli sia dipingere tutto quello, che il capriccio gli detta; con
quei gesti, con quei sforzi sieno però convenevoli a la figura,
che egli fa." In the course of the next two pages Gilio
translates a number of lines from the famous beginning of
the *Ars poetica* in which Horace remarks that poets and
painters have always had liberty of imagination, but that
poets—and Gilio means that these lines shall apply as well
to painters—must not make savage mate with tame, or
serpents with birds, etc. (see note 14).

172. There were very rare "fintioni concesse," but only,
it would seem, if these could be construed to have some
bearing of their own on theological truth. See note 168.

173. *Ibid.*, p. 116.

174. *Ibid.*, p. 117.

175. *Ibid.*: "Però i Cristiani da questi esempi mossi
hanno imparato a dar forma humana a la Religione, a la
Fede, a la Speranza, a la Carità, ed a l'altre virtù che
insieme con queste vanno mescolatamente con le cose sacre,
e virtù Teologiche si chiamano; non per altro fra le
cose sacre si mettono, che per esser virtù, come che la
purita de la religione altro che cose virtuose non richieda,
e spetialmente queste."

176. See p. 22 and note 86.

But a few allegorical figures, and only because they are sanctioned by antique example, are almost the sole deviation from factual truth that the jealous theologians will allow in religious painting,[177] and they can hardly be said to afford much scope to the imagination. Otherwise the painter of religious subjects is, as we have seen, one who paints the literal facts of history, and it is evident that he must have sufficient learning, let alone orthodox habits of mind, to paint pictures that will pass muster with the most uncompromising theologians. The concept that a painter like a poet must be learned in the interest of decorum, will be discussed later. Here it may be further observed that criticism like Gilio's, although it shows no interest whatsoever· in formal beauty and evinces in its theological pedantry a painful misunderstanding of the grandeur of Michelangelo's profoundly personal interpretation of his subject, has nevertheless this much to be said in its favor: when Gilio asserts that the immoderate contortions of Michelangelo's angels are to display the power of art (*la forza d'arte*),[178] and that Michelangelo has not erred through ignorance, but through a desire to serve art rather than the truths of religion,[179] he strikes not merely ᶜat the manneristic extravagance of Michelangelo's late style, but, what is more important, through Michelangelo at the general tendency in Mannerist art to sacrifice meaning to empty aestheticism. And in one of the most interesting of a number of passages in Gilio's book that might serve as texts for a lecture on the aesthetic extravagance of the Mannerist style, the author, after remarking that errors of fact in painting are due to ignorance and might be avoided if the painters were only men of letters and took the trouble to inform themselves about their subjects, adds that "they appear to think that they have paid their debt when they have made a saint and have put all their genius and diligence into twisting awry the legs, or the arms, or the neck; and in a violent manner that is both unseemly and ugly."[180] Through the dark glass, therefore, of crabbed and impercipient clericalism one may discern in Gilio not only the need of a deeper religious content in human life, but also the aesthetic need that the Baroque style later attempted to satisfy, of more adequate forms of expression.[181]

The dialogue is further significant as indicating along with other documents of the time[182] the temporary impoverishment of humanistic values that accompanied the breakdown of the Classical Renaissance in the sixteenth century, and the policy of the Church to press the arts into the service of morality and Christian dogma. For the student of the theory *ut pictura poesis*, it is illuminating as showing how the concept of artistic decorum which in Horace's own mind was not devoid of moral implication, could acquire under particular historical conditions a dogmatic significance in which its classical connotations of representative truth were entirely lost. Painting, since its content was that of poetry,

---

177. See note 172.

178. *Op. cit.*, p. 90.

179. *Ibid.*, p. 101: "Credo certo che Michelagnolo ... per ignoranza non ha errato, ma piu tosto ha voluto abbellire il pennello, e compiacere a l'arte che al vero. Io penso certo, che piu sarebbe piaciuto, ed ammirato se questo mistero fatto havesse come l'historia richiedeva che come l'ha fatto."

180. *Op. cit.*, p. 84: "E se fussero considerati come dianzi diceste in fare i modelli, gli schizzi, i cartoni, informarsi bene d'ogni cosa, non gli avverrebbe questo; e par loro haver pagato il debito, quando hanno fatto un santo; e haver messo tutto l'ingegno, e la diligenza in torcerli le gambe, ò le braccia, ò'l collo torto; e farlo sforzato, di sforzo sconvenevole e brutto."

181. Despite his criticism of Michelangelo, Gilio pays tribute to him (*ibid.*, p. 110) because at a time when painting was lifeless (all the other sciences also being lifeless) he

"non solo ha rilevata la quasi perduta scienza; ma l'ha in modo abbellita, ed à perfettione ridotta, che non possiamo haver invidia a gli antichi, e l'ha tanto col suo sapere illustrata, che se non passa aguaglia quella, per la quale gli Apelli, Timagori, i Zeusi, i Protogeni, i Pulignoti, e gli altri ne sono chiari e famosi al mondo. Onde dir possiamo, se egli stato non fusse sarebbe quasi di mano à gli artefici uscita." It is typical of the spiritual cross-currents of the century that Gilio should praise Michelangelo as the equal of the ancients just after he has condemned him severely for religious indecorum. In a later passage Raphael (*ibid.*, p. 116) is also included as one who helped bring art back to the fair estate which it had enjoyed among the ancients, but he receives no such praise as Michelangelo does here.

182. See the reference to Ammanati's famous letter of 1582 in note 157. It is published in Bottari, *Raccolta di lettere*, Milan, 1822, III, 532–39.

and since its effects on human emotion were the same, was subject to the same laws of decorum; and if it dealt with religious subjects, it had accordingly to be a categorically exact, as well as a vivid and moving, illustration of the facts of Christian history and the truths of theology. This specialized application of the Horatian concept did not outlast the Mannerist period, but it helped to encourage the view that persisted in the following century that decorum implied not only representative truth, but truth that was morally edifying as well. Herein for the seventeenth century, as for Horace, lay its connection with the precept that art should instruct as well as delight. In the preface to his *Conférences de l'Académie* Félibien, for instance, regarded decorum (*bienséance*) as "one of the most necessary elements in painting to instruct the ignorant, and one of the most agreeable in the eyes of the learned."[183]

That it might well be both is apparent from his remarks on decorum that immediately precede this thoroughly Horatian observation. For they reveal that close connection between learning and the ability to render things with strict appropriateness already remarked in Gilio da Fabriano. "Decorum must be observed," writes Félibien, out-Horacing Horace, "in regard to ages, sexes, countries, different professions, manners and customs, passions, and usages of dress appropriate to each nation. Herein is Raphael admirable, but not so Titian and Veronese."[184] The formalistic implications of a passage like this—and one will immediately think of the aridly conventional gestures and expression of much French painting of the late seventeenth century—are sufficiently obvious. It is clear, moreover, that if the artist is successfully to observe decorum in its diverse ramifications, he must get his facts straight about a great variety of men and nations, both ancient and modern; he must in short be possessed of a truly uncommon erudition. Hence it is that the critics frequently undertake to instruct the painters in what they must know if they are to be historical painters worthy of the name. What they tell them, often at great length, Boileau, instructing the poet concerning decorum, sums up in three lines:

> Conservez à chacun son propre caractère.
> Des siècles, des pais, étudiez les mœurs,
> Les climats font souvent les diverses humeurs.[185]

VI—THE LEARNED PAINTER

The theory of the learned painter, twin brother of the learned poet whose prototype was the *doctus poeta* of antiquity, was an important element in the doctrine *ut pictura poesis*. Furthermore it was an element of great vitality which, gathering girth and momentum in the sixteenth century, had hardly spent its energy by the end of the eighteenth. Yet as fashioned by the Italian critics of the Cinquecento, the learned painter is a highly theoretical personage who, if he cannot be called an actual figment of the imagination, has never had more than a partial basis in reality; and much of the time he has had no basis there at all. Now no sympathetic student of the Renaissance will quarrel with the view already expressed in the fifteenth century by Alberti that the painter will do well to know the poets and historians who will supply him with subjects of universal interest, and to associate with poets and learned men of his own day and age who may provide interesting ideas.[186] But when in the later sixteenth century it is also insisted—and critics of literature were giving the same advice to the poet—that the painter be learned not only in sacred and profane

183. P. 317.
184. *Loc. cit.*

185. *L'art poétique*, III, 113-15.
186. See Chapter II and notes 73 and 74.

literature, but also in geography, climatology, geology, theology, and the manners and customs of various countries, for only with a fund of precise knowledge can a painter show the proper respect for those poetical and historical texts, often hallowed by antiquity or religion, which provide him with his subject matter; when the critics have thus elevated the painter to the rank of *maestro di color che sanno*—and Bellori actually applies to Raphael Dante's famous characterization of Aristotle[187]—one is aware that pedantry has intruded on good sense.

It has already been noted in the discussion of Gilio da Fabriano's estimate of Michelangelo's *Last Judgment* that the critics associated a painter's observance of decorum with his knowledge of texts; for a violation of historical truth taken in its broadest sense to include the events of religious narrative, might mean in the latter case religious impropriety, or with other subject matter, the incongruity now slight, now serious enough to occasion loss of universal truth, that anachronism is likely to bring in its train. But in point of fact decorum (taken in its most inclusive sense to mean the observance in any subject of seriousness or magnitude of a certain propriety, not only for the sake of representative truth but also in one sense or another of decency or good form), although it will always depend to some extent on avoiding the picturesque use of contemporary costume and setting at the expense of emphasis on universal human content, simply does not depend on that total avoidance of the local and contemporary that the critics thought an accurate observance of texts would insure. In spite of the contemporary dress of the apostles and servants and the presence of a small dog under the table, no sensible critic of today would say, for instance, that Titian's *Supper at Emmaus* in the Louvre lacks decorum; for although the painter has given the religious theme a patrician character that is not in keeping with the Gospel, he has nevertheless treated it with becoming reverence and dignity. And with all due respect to Félibien who remarked, as we have seen, that Titian lacked decorum, genuine decorum in a picture depends not on the presence or absence of the realistic and contemporary, but on the painter's treatment of these elements. It depends, that is, on his personal attitude towards his subject which is embodied in his style, and one may say truly that if the dog under the table in Titian's *Supper at Emmaus* were prominently displayed as he is in Veronese's painting of the same subject—a painting, by the way, in which the French Academy, this time with good reason, refused to admit the existence of decorum[188]—or if the contemporary dress or landscape instead of taking their places easily in the monumental pattern of the picture intruded in any self-assertive manner on the importance and dignity of the human content, then to speak of indecorum might be justified. And that would be to admit that decorum is actually far more a matter of the artist's point of view as reflected in his style than of adherence to the truth of historical detail, and to give the lie to those sixteenth-century critics who in self-defense would have had logically and foolishly to declare that the decorum of the picture would at least be improved had the painter displayed a knowledge of Palestinian dress, architecture, landscape, and tableware of the first century A.D.

This is perhaps an overstatement of the case, but it is not without its foundation in

187. *Idea*, p. 6.
188. In the *Conférence* of October 1, 1667, in which Nocret discussed the picture, today in the Louvre, concentrating on its fine composition and color and generally abstaining from a discussion of the higher virtues of the historical painter in which Veronese in the Academy's eyes was obviously lacking. Some who attended the discussion attempted to justify all the well-dressed people in the picture who do not appear in the Bible on the ground that they might have been in the place where the disciples and Christ were to eat supper, and seeing something remarkable in Christ, have remained to look at him. But the Academy refused to accept this "charitable excuse" and, for obvious reasons, to discuss decorum further (see Jouin, *Conférences*, p. 47).

fact in the writing of the sixteenth century. Dolce, for instance, declares that for decorum's sake the painter must not only represent a traditional figure like Moses with due grandeur and majesty, but must also on all occasions "take into account the rank of the persons whom he will represent, and not less, the nations, customs, places and epochs: so that if he will paint a feat of arms of Caesar or of Alexander the Great, it would not be appropriate to arm the soldiers as they would be armed today; and in the one case he will depict Macedonian arms and, in the other, Roman; and if it shall be his task to represent a modern battle, he must not seek to dispose it in the antique manner. By the same tokens, if he wishes to represent Caesar, it would be ridiculous to put a Turkish turban on his head, or one of our caps, or yet one in the Venetian style."[189] And shortly thereafter he adds: "Not less must the painter fashion localities and buildings according to the nature of the countries in which they are found so that he will not attribute to one country what is appropriate to another. Wherefore that painter was not very wise who, when he painted Moses striking the rock with his rod and causing the water desired by the Hebrews miraculously to issue forth, imagined a country fertile, grassy, and girt with charming hills: because history has it that this miracle happened in the desert; and besides, in fertile places there is always plenty of water."[190] Now one will readily admit that in a subject of this sort the fertility and beauty of the countryside should not receive undue emphasis. Nevertheless, Dolce's remarks are an example of that literal reading of a picture at the expense of its significant dramatic content that criticism in the name of decorum, or perhaps of verisimilitude,[191] or simply of learning for its own sake, would for two centuries seek to encourage. And it is interesting to read in the *Poetica* of Daniello, published some twenty years before Dolce's treatise, a similar injunction to the poet to encompass in his mind a vast and diverse erudition; for since human and divine events are his province, the poet must have knowledge "if not of all sciences and doctrines, at least of the greater part" and this comprehensive requirement includes more specifically the principles of supernatural, natural, and moral philosophy (for *il sapere*, and here he translates Horace, *è principio e fonte dello scrivere bene*) of which the great Latin and modern poets are the repositories and which must, however, be supplemented by a "very wide experience of things that are done on land and sea"; and this practical experience of the nature of things includes within its own gigantic boundaries not only an expert knowledge of the conduct of land and naval warfare, but also the customs, modes of living, and habits of different peoples; "to put it briefly," as Daniello says with unconscious humor, "everything that has to do with the practical living of life."[192]

The reader with the leisure to compare the treatises of Daniello and Dolce will encounter a striking similarity between them not merely in their insistence on the erudition of poet and painter, but in the order which they observe in developing their theories, and in their specific comments on invention, decorum, the purpose of art, and the like.[193] Daniello's book, published in Venice in 1536, was of course readily accessible to Dolce, and it is not improbable that the latter modeled the general form of his theoretical exposition on that of the *Poetica*. In any event, it is scarcely hyperbole to say that in extended passages in both books a substitution of the word painter for poet, or vice versa, as the case required, would make no important difference in the sense. This fact alone, even if one ignored all the knowledge of Horace and Aristotle that Dolce patently displays, would give ample

---

189. *Dialogo della pittura*, p. 154.
190. *Ibid.*, p. 162.
191. See Appendix 6, "Decorum and Verisimilitude."

192. P. 34: "tutte quelle cose che d'intorno alla pratica consistono."
193. See Appendices 2, 3; notes 73, 92, 145.

measure of the extent to which the doctrine *ut pictura poesis* was, alike in its origins and in its sixteenth-century development, a purely literary theory that a writer of humanistic temper could genially transfer to the sister art. But to return to Dolce's learned painter who finds his close parallel in Daniello's learned poet, it is interesting to see how at the end of the sixteenth century the critics influenced by the Counter-Reform exhort the painter to be well read above all in ecclesiastical literature. A painter dare not be ignorant of sacred history, writes Lomazzo in his last book, nor of matters pertaining to theology which he can at least learn by conversation with theologians; thus he will know how he should represent heaven and hell and their inhabitants; nor are the legends of the saints to be neglected.[194] Sacred literature then comes first, displacing the poetry of an earlier day, and Lomazzo's list that follows deserves some comment.[195] As one who had been a practicing artist he insists upon geometry and perspective which Dolce, as a cultivated connoisseur but no painter, did not; and on music and architecture, and on history which must be treated with absolute truth. Poetry appears rather ingloriously near the end of the list—further evidence of the temporary eclipse of humanism in the late Cinquecento—although Lomazzo is aware in a passage that has the familiar Horatian ring that painter and poet are most alike in possessing freedom of imagination (*la licenza del fingere e inventare*); and that a knowledge of poetry adds charm to the painter's inventions. After this rather conventional concession to the value of humane studies which seems to come almost as an afterthought, as if Lomazzo had suddenly remembered the humanistic compliments to painting in his earlier treatise,[196] he abruptly reverts to the Leonardesque by declaring that anatomy is more important to the painter than aught else. But he seems again to recall his earlier writing on expression when he observes that painters must know the "affetti humani" to which he had devoted a whole book of his earlier treatise, not to mention a round fifty pages of quotations from the poets, chiefly Ariosto, and the recently published *Gerusalemme liberata*, that might serve as touchstones for the painters in their own rendering of human emotions.[197] No one will object to Lomazzo's scientific requirements for the painter wherein he remembers Leonardo and Alberti, nor certainly what mention he makes of liberal studies. But it is the totality of the program, let alone the fact that it is set down as a program at all, that is appalling; and it should be remembered that Lomazzo's insistence on unmitigated accuracy in the rendering of history—such accuracy would be the logical result of the learned program—is the general point of view of the sixteenth century from Dolce onward. Very gratuitously Borghini makes assurance doubly sure by enjoining a like strictness in the rendering of fables from the poets, taking Titian seriously to task for a misreading of Ovid and others in a painting of Venus and Adonis.[198] Thus the painter, no matter what his source, must quote literally both chapter and verse.

The pedantry of the sixteenth-century critics was fortunately not so labored in the age of French classicism, but the critics still insisted in all sincerity that a painter must be a learned man and abide by the truth of the written word. Fréart de Chambray's first two rules for decorous composition are "that in Historical Composures the pure and rigid truth be always religiously observed"—a clear echo of the piety of the Counter-Reform—and

---

194. *Idea*, p. 33.
195. *Ibid.*, pp. 34–37. See in note 73 Armenini's list of books that the painter should read, and cf. the long list of De Piles in his commentary on Du Fresnoy (Dryden's translation, pp. 111 ff.).
196. See Appendix 3 and note 75.
197. *Trattato*, VI, 65, pp. 487 ff.
198. *Il riposo*, p. 49: "Perchè da essi è detto, che Adone,

quando fu pregato da Venere, sele gittò ginocchioni a'piedi, ringraziandola d'essersi degnata di conceder la sua divina bellezza a uomo mortale e che era presto con riverenza a fare ogni suo piacere; per questo pare, che Tiziano nell'invenzione abbia mancato, fingendo Adone da Venere, che sta in atto di abbracciarlo, fuggire; dove egli molto disiderava i suoi abbracciamenti." The painting is in the Prado.

"that there be great consideration had of the place where 'tis to be represented."[199] John Dryden flatly tells painters and poets alike to follow texts of ancient authors,[200] and the famous English connoisseur and traveler John Evelyn, who translated Fréart de Chambray, remarks that the best painters are "learned men, good historians and [note the English touch!] generally skilled in the best antiquities," after which there follows a list of learned artists including Alberti, Rubens, Poussin, and finally Bernini, "who on one occasion built the theater, cut the figures, painted the scenes, wrote the play and composed the music." Evelyn then hastens to add patriotically that Sir Christopher Wren could have done even better had he tried![201]

Félibien pays tribute to Poussin's historical sense when he remarks in a passage certainly reminiscent of one lately quoted from Dolce that the great painters "did not fall into the errors and gross examples of ignorance of those painters who represent in fair and verdant landscapes actions that took place in arid and desert countries; who confound sacred history with fable, who clothe the ancient Greeks and Romans in modern dress";[202] and that Poussin himself was eager to observe historical truth appears in his reaction, recorded by Félibien, to some criticism of one of his paintings of *Moses Striking the Water from the Rock*. Some stickler for pictorial accuracy had remarked that the bed in which the stream of water flowed could not have become so deep in so little time, nor could nature have so ordained matters in a place so dry and arid as the desert. But Poussin responded in kind and defended himself by saying that he was "well enough instructed in what is permitted a painter in those things which he will represent, which can be taken and considered as they have been, as they still are, or as they ought to be:[203] that so far as he could see, the disposition of the place where the miracle took place ought to be of the sort that he depicted, because otherwise the water could not have been gathered together nor made use of in the need that so great a number of people had of it, but would have spread abroad on all sides."[204] This is an example of the casuistry in which in the name of historical truth the critics and even so intelligent a painter as Poussin were prone to indulge. That it has little to do with the final evaluation of a work of art is sufficiently obvious, and it should be again recorded to the credit of the French Academy that on some occasions at least, it justified Poussin for having taken liberties with historical fact because in so doing, it was argued, he attained a higher truth. Thus when he was accused of having violated truth in his painting of *Eliezer and Rebecca* by omitting the ten camels required by the biblical narrative,[205] Le Brun defended him, maintaining that he had showed great discrimination thereby; for by dispensing with what was dramatically irrelevant he had focused the interest of the spectator on the principal subject, and this he could not have done had a quantity of unlovely camels been present to debauch the eye. Furthermore, a whole caravan of camels in such a subject would have been a mingling of the comic with the serious quite as unwarranted as a mingling of contrary modes in music. Thus when Poussin omitted the camels, not only did he fail to violate history in any important sense, but his painting gained in unity of action and in decorum. And to clinch his argument Le Brun made the inevitable

199. Roland Fréart, Sieur de Chambray, *An Idea of the Perfection of Painting*, trans. John Evelyn, London, 1668, p. 72 (first French ed. 1662). His third rule is "that one never discover those Parts and Members of the body which cannot honestly be exposed," a clear echo of the piety of the Counter-Reform that recalls Lomazzo. Cf. note 157.

200. See the preface to his translation of Du Fresnoy, p. xxxviii.

201. Preface to his translation of Fréart de Chambray.

202. *Entretien* no. 8, IV, 93.

203. ". . . comme elles ont été, comme elles sont encore, ou comme elles doivent être;" Poussin seems here to have confused Aristotle with a temporal notion. Cf. notes 12, 64.

204. Félibien, *op. cit.*, pp. 60–61.

205. In Philippe de Champaigne's well-known analysis before the Academy of the picture today in the Louvre (see Jouin, *op. cit.*, pp. 93–95).

appeal to the sister art of poetry, quoting Poussin to the effect that poetry no more than painting allows the easy and familiar expression of comedy to be mingled with the pomp and gravity of the heroic.

But although the concept of the painter as an accurate historian could thus be subjected to intelligent criticism among the Academicians, and for several decades after the death of Le Brun was to decline in influence among the best painters, it persisted in criticism.[206] And in 1748 when Charles Coypel attempted to restore the Academy to the learned position of its brave days under Le Brun,[207] it was revived with new energy. It was not, however, a concept that would ultimately survive the impact of Rousseau on European thought, and although Delacroix was a distinguished and learned painter of fable whose journals bear witness to his belief in some important elements in the doctrine *ut pictura poesis*, he was cool to the notion that vast learning was essential for the painter, believing rightly that a thorough knowledge of the techniques and traditions of his own art were far more important.[208] But before the eighteenth century had ended, Reynolds with his usual good sense had divested the academic tradition which in the main he championed, of the nonsense of the learned painter, and with it much of the nonsense of decorum. Speaking of that "solid science" on which the art of painting is founded he remarks:

> Some writers upon art carry this point too far and suppose that such a body of universal and profound learning is requisite, that the very enumeration of its kinds is enough to frighten a beginner. Vitruvius after going through the many accomplishments of nature, and the many acquirements of learning, necessary to an architect, proceeds with great gravity to assert that he ought to be well skilled in the civil law, that he may not be cheated in the title of the ground he builds on. But without such exaggeration we may go so far as to assert that a painter stands in need of more knowledge than is to be picked off his palette, or collected by looking on his model, whether it be in life or in picture. He can never be a great artist who is grossly illiterate.[209]

This is sensible middle ground and a *caveat* alike to academic pedantry and to untutored expressionism.

The idea of the encyclopedic painter has never among the great painters, and rarely at that, had more than an approximation in fact. Poussin who "transports us to the environs of ancient Rome with all the objects which a literary [and, Reynolds should have added, an archaeological] education makes so precious and interesting to man,"[210] comes as close as any, and even when the scenes of his paintings were laid in foreign places that he had never seen, he was frequently careful to include some distinguishing mark that would identify the country in which the event took place. Thus in scenes laid in Egypt he would often add a pyramid or an obelisk to an architecture that he otherwise based on classical or medieval forms, or a palm tree to his usual foliage;[211] and for the painting of the *Virgin in Egypt* made for Mme de Chantelou he tells us himself that for a procession of priests, and

206. Antoine Coypel in 1721 advises the painter to be instructed in history, in geography, in the variety of manners, religions, customs and dress, in the places where countries, seas and climates are found, adding that "the books of the voyagers will teach him the diversity of buildings, trees, animals, and of different characters necessary to expression" (see Jouin, *op. cit.*, p. 333).

207. See J. Locquin, *La peinture d'histoire en France*, Paris, 1912, pp. 3–13, pp. 87 ff.

208. *Journal*, ed. Joubin, Paris, 1932, III, 24.

209. *Discourse* VII, December 10, 1776. Reynolds goes on to say with Alberti, Lomazzo, and others that the painter must be "tolerably conversant with the poets in

some language or other that he may imbibe a poetical spirit and enlarge his stock of ideas"; that he should compare and digest his notions, and not be wholly unacquainted with that part of philosophy which gives an insight into human nature. "He ought to know *something* concerning the mind, as well as *a great deal* concerning the body of man." (The italics are Reynolds'.)

210. *Discourse* XIII.

211. Pointed out by Du Bos, *Réflexions critiques*, I, 30, p. 274; see, for instance, the *Finding of the Infant Moses* of 1647 in the Louvre (illustrated in W. Friedlaender, *Nicolas Poussin*, Munich, 1914, p. 228; cf. p. 119).

other Egyptian local color, he had availed himself of the natural and moral history of the Egyptians displayed in the mosaic pavement of the Temple of Fortune in Palestrina.[212] And we have already seen that he could take an imputation of factual inaccuracy in his painting seriously enough to argue the point in an effort to prove himself a good historian. Yet for all his Roman learning and his conscientiousness he was far from being elaborately learned in what was called the science of *costume*[213]—that exact knowledge of the habits, customs, and local color of various peoples and countries, that the critics in the name of decorum or verisimilitude insisted upon as necessary to the painter of history. To be so he would have had to travel to other lands than Italy, as Delacroix and Decamps were to do in the nineteenth century, when curiously enough the Romantic Movement encouraged exact reproduction of the scene and dress of foreign lands that were far closer to what the academic critics of the sixteenth and seventeenth centuries demanded than anything produced in their own time. But always in his great histories, and even in those cases in which, as we have just seen, he attempted to locate his scene geographically, Poussin's landscape, architecture, and dress are generalizations based on Italian or on classical forms with which the exact science of *costume* has little to do, and in which even his Roman learning is entirely subsumed. And this subordination of learning to artistic creation was as inevitable in Poussin as it must be in any great and learned painter who sees the forms of nature or the actions of men under the aspect of eternity. A less profound spirit like Le Brun who held by the rules and sponsored an academic program might, as Du Bos tells us, have someone draw Persian horses for him at Aleppo in order that he might observe *costume* in his histories of Alexander.[214] But if one turns to the great painters of the Renaissance who flourished before the doctrine of the learned painter developed, certainly it is true that when they illustrated the fables of the poets or subjects from history or scripture they were never, for all their association with humanists, primarily scholars themselves, nor concerned primarily with the scrupulous following of texts; but treated their literary material freely and imaginatively, adapting it to the possibilities of their own medium of expression and to the traditional language of their own art. Thus, one may repeat, the learned, nay pedantic painter, was never so much an actuality as he was an idea whom the sixteenth-century critics created far more in their own image than on the basis of knowledge actually revealed by the great painters in their art—some of whom, as we have seen, they occasionally took to task for what one might call their misquotation of poetic or historical texts. It is not surprising that this theory should first evolve in a century that saw a decline in the creative energy both of art and scholarship; and like much of the Mannerist art of the period it is a distortion of objective truth. What several critics required of the sixteenth-century painter in the way of erudition we have already seen. And from 1550 to 1750 a host of passages might be quoted in which the mantle of poet, historian, or sage, is made to descend upon the painter's innocent shoulders or in which he is enjoined to deal accurately with the printed word. Near the end of the critical tradition of the Renaissance the eighteenth-century English painter and critic, Jonathan Richardson, who was respected in his day, after remarking on the universal language of painting (by which he

---

212. Letter to Chantelou of November 25, 1658 (Jouanny, p. 448). See Friedlaender, *op. cit.*, p. 123 and drawing on p. 257. Rubens' antiquarian interests also led him to be conscientious in matters of historical detail, and he was praised for his historical exactitude even to the rendering of the nails in the boots of one of the chevaliers in a painting of the Constantine series. Professor A. M.

Friend has called my attention to Peiresc's letter to Rubens in which this praise is recorded (see M. Rooses, *L'œuvre de P. P. Rubens*, Antwerp, 1890, III, 217).

213. See Félibien, Preface, p. 317, and Du Bos in Appendix 6.

214. *Op. cit.*, p. 275.

means its appeal to the sense of sight), makes the amazing observation that "men of all nations hear the poet, moralist, historian, divine, or whatever other character the painter assumes, speaking to them in their own mother tongue."[215] One may be permitted to ask whether the painter may not also assume the character of painter; and it may not be inappropriate to observe in this connection that Leonardo da Vinci two centuries before, near the beginning of Renaissance criticism, had strenuously objected to the poet on precisely the same grounds that Richardson near the end of the Renaissance tradition approves the painter, namely that the poet poaches so much on the alien territory of scientists, theologians, and philosophers that he may be said scarcely to exist in his character of poet at all.[216] And it is probable that Leonardo, enamored of the sense of sight, and seeing in the painter's art only direct and vivid imitation of nature uncontaminated by adventitious learning, would have regarded the doctrine of the erudite painter with a mortal disgust.

VII—RINALDO AND ARMIDA

In the last chapter an attempt was made to demonstrate how artificial is the doctrine of the learned painter. And it may be further put to the test and found wanting, if one considers the illustration of a celebrated episode from Tasso's famous epic, the *Gerusalemme liberata*, that began to supply subjects for the painters some ten or fifteen years after its publication in 1581. It is hardly necessary to remark that the painter-illustrators of Tasso's poem of necessity fulfilled some of the more important tenets of the doctrine *ut pictura poesis*. In choosing subjects from an epic poem of high seriousness in which heroic history was mingled with the marvelous, they shared the poet's great invention, and like him were imitators of human action of more than common interest and significance. Expression, in which, according to Lomazzo, painting chiefly resembles poetry, would depend on the genius of the painter and on his interest in the human emotion portrayed in the poem. Decorum, a formalistic notion that was not likely, as we have seen, to make for freshness and originality, he would do well to leave to the critics, as indeed he generally did. He was equally unaware, it would seem, of the precept that painting like poetry should instruct as well as delight, for he resolutely eschewed the serious main action of the poem that had to do with the siege and capture of Jerusalem under the crusader Godfrey of Boulogne, and chose for the most part only those amorous and idyllic episodes wherein the lyric element is strong, and Tasso's idiosyncratic vein of tender melancholy finds unfettered expression. And his treatment of these could scarcely be said to disclose didactic intent. Such are the episodes of Erminia, the pagan princess, taking up her abode with the shepherds amid the simple pleasures of the country far from the iniquity of courts, and of Rinaldo's enchantment in the Fortunate Isles by the beautiful witch Armida, famous for its langorous voluptuousness. These subjects were immediately popular not only for their intrinsic beauty and human interest, but also because they had behind them a long tradition of pastoral art and literature extending back into antiquity, with its images of the country, its implications of escape from the weary, complex life of cities, and its haunting references to the Golden Age when an idly happy life prevailed. And such current erotic mythologies among the Renaissance painters as Venus and Adonis, AuroraandCephalus, or Diana and Endymion, and the general popularity of Ovid, helped to prepare particularly for the enthusiastic reception accorded the story of Rinaldo and Armida.

215. "Essay on the Art of Criticism" in *Works of Mr. Jonathan Richardson*, London, 1773, p. 2 (first ed. 1719).

216. *Trattato*, I, 14, 23 (near end).

We shall now consider briefly some aspects of the pictorial treatment of this episode.[217] And it should be very clearly stated at the beginning that the painters who illustrated Tasso's story were not the conscientious scholars that the critics for the sake of decorum or verisimilitude would have them be. For they not only took liberties with the text when pictorial exigency required it, as they were generally forbidden to do by the critics, but also employed traditional forms of composition or iconography that had served the painters and sculptors of antiquity or their own Renaissance predecessors for illustration of fables that, more often than not, bore some similarity to various episodes in Tasso's poem. Here was the use of another kind of knowledge that the critics, even while urging a thorough knowledge of the antique, and of the best art of the moderns, with their strong literary predilections scarcely took into account: a knowledge that the painter does not acquire from books, but from association with the traditional language of the arts of representation that his genius is forever evoking into new possibilities of composition and of interpretation.

The first scene in the episode, as it appears in Poussin's version in Moscow, represents Armida falling in love with Rinaldo as he lies asleep on the bank of the river Orontes (Fig. 2). As she bends over to kill the Christian warrior who is her mortal enemy, her hate is suddenly transformed into love.[218] Now Poussin, who was in conscious sympathy with the humanistic doctrine *ut pictura poesis*, could be expected in his pictorial rendering of such an episode to be reasonably faithful to the spirit of his text, and he has even been careful, in addition to rendering Rinaldo in armor which would distinguish him from an Adonis or Endymion in a similar grouping,[219] to display at the right, as unmistakable means of identifying the subject, the column that bore the legend enjoining Rinaldo to discover the hidden marvels of the island in the midst of the river.[220] Poussin might indeed have pleased some of the critics by including as other painters did the nymphs whose song enchanted Rinaldo into slumber;[221] but these from considerations of formal composition and dramatic effectiveness he evidently rejected as superfluous to his composition. He might have satisfied an extreme purist among the critics by indicating that he had studied the geography and dress of Syria after the manner of the nineteenth-century romantic painters. But this would have been to call attention to adventitious and local detail at the expense of universal truth. Poussin's naturally abstemious genius, fortified by the teaching of antiquity, necessarily rejected any such conformity with pedantic theorizing; and for the student of *ut pictura poesis*, the influence of antiquity on this painting is particularly illuminating.

The picture dates between 1635 and 1640[222] and may be the earliest example of a scene never popular among Italian painters. It shows Poussin using various features of the story of Endymion which he could have seen represented on several antique sarcophagi in Rome during the years of his life there. A drawing by Poussin in Chantilly of a sarcophagus

217. I am engaged at present in preparing a book on the influence of this poem and of Ariosto's *Orlando Furioso* on the history of painting, in which the illustration of this episode will be treated with greater completeness.

218. Canto XIV, stanzas 65–67:

"Esce d'agguato allor la falsa maga,
E gli va sopra, di vendetta vaga.
  Ma quando in lui fissò lo sguardo, e vide
Come placido in vista egli respira,
E ne'begli occhi un dolce atto che ride,
Ben che sian chiusi (or che fia s'ei li gira?)
Pria s'arresta sospesa, e gli s'asside
Poscia vicina, e placar sente ogn'ira
Mentre il risguarda; e in su la vaga fronte
Pende omai sì, che par Narciso al fonte.

E quei ch'ivi sorgean vivi sudori
Accoglie lievemente in un suo velo;
E, con un dolce ventilar, gli ardori
Gli va temprando de l'estivo cielo
Così (chi'l crederia?) sopiti ardori
D'occhi nascosi distemprâr quel gelo
Che s'indurava al cor più che diamante;
E, di nemica, ella divenne amante."

219. As in Poussin's own *Death of Adonis* in the Museum of Caen. See O. Grautoff, *Nicolas Poussin*, Munich, 1914, II, pl. 34.

220. Canto XIV, stanzas 57–58.

221. Simon Vouet painted such a version (see note 228).

222. See Friedlaender, *op. cit.*, p. 51.

already known in the second decade of the seventeenth century (Fig. 3)[223] illustrates the nightly visit of Selene to the Latmian shepherd who slumbers supported by the figure of Somnus. Here are already several elements of the Moscow composition: the sleeping figure with the left arm raised and bent as the hand supports the head; the left leg drawn up to repeat the angle of the bent arm; the chariot and horses with the female figure of Aura holding the bridle; and the attendant putti. The figure of Selene stepping from her chariot advances towards the sleeping Endymion, while in the Moscow picture Poussin, respecting Tasso's fable and sentiment, represents Armida bending over Rinaldo, her gaze fixed on his sleeping face. Another Endymion sarcophagus,[224] represented here by a drawing from the Dal Pozzo collection (Fig. 5), shows the horses rearing and the figure of Aura dynamically posed as in Poussin's painting, while a third example (Fig. 6) shows a like variety of comparable elements:[225] Selene at the right supported by a female figure about to bend over the sleeping Endymion; the chariot in the center, in this case with the unusual substitution of bulls for horses; the seated female figure behind—Robert calls her Venus—who, with her flying garment, and in the counterpoise of her figure as she swings her head in the direction of the central event, resembles the figure seated on the horse in Poussin's picture; and finally the reclining figure of Oceanus at the feet of Aura who may be compared with Poussin's personification of the river Orontes. This last sarcophagus not only displays all of the figure elements employed by Poussin in comparable poses, but the central triangle dominated by the figure of Venus, with the two reclining figures that balance one another at its base, also resembles Poussin's triangular composition. Now it is of course possible that Poussin could have found individual figures with poses similar to those in his picture on a variety of antique monuments, but he found practically all that he needed on the Endymion sarcophagi alone which illustrated, moreover, a love story in which the incident of the woman leaving her chariot to approach her sleeping lover is similar to the episode from Tasso's poem. It is therefore reasonable to conclude that Poussin, sensitive to content, and learned not only in the fables of the poets but also—and this was of equal significance for his art—in the iconographic tradition of the visual arts, found in antique representations of the story of Endymion precisely the materials that he needed for his pictorial treatment of a new literary subject. Thus as often in his work, the imaginative use of ancient imagery for new pictorial purposes carries with it, in subtly evoking the ancient myth, a poetic richness of overtone; and the antique language of form, unobtrusively adapted to new expressive uses, maintains a palpable and eloquent continuity. And it is interesting to observe that although the antique components of the depiction of the myth of Endymion served Poussin for the episode of Rinaldo and Armida, when he came to represent the myth itself, as in the beautiful Detroit picture (Fig. 7), he abandoned, as if unwilling to plagiarize, the elements on the Endymion sarcophagi; and in his highly original representation of Selene's departure from Endymion who kneels at her feet as the horses of the sun bring up the dawn—a scene so far as I know never appearing in ancient art—he combines in a spirit of free invention other plastic elements from the art of the distant past.[226] Nothing perhaps could better

223. Now set into the outer wall of the Palazzo Rospigliosi. See C. Robert, *Die antiken Sarkophag-Reliefs*, Berlin, 1890–1919, III, Part 1, p. 66; pl. XIII, fig. 47.

224. A fragment now exists in the Palazzo Farnese. See *ibid.*, p. 90; cf. pl. XIX, fig. 75.

225. In the wall of the cloister of San Paolo fuori-le-mura. See *ibid.*, p. 101; pl. XXIII, fig. 81. There is no reason to suppose that it was not there in Poussin's time.

226. Cf. for instance the figure of Selene with the figure of Artemis in a wall painting in Stabiae (Reinach, *Repertoire des peintures grecques et romaines*, Paris, 1922, p. 52, fig. 1). The figure drawing aside the curtain is a plain adaptation of the common Hellenistic type represented in the Victory of Brescia, the Capuan Aphrodite in Naples, etc. The sleeping figure and the sun god with his horses are obvious classical motives.

illustrate Poussin's profound and subtle originality than a comparison of the methods employed in composing these two paintings.

If we consider the succeeding episodes of the story of Rinaldo and Armida as interpreted by the painters, more and more material comes to hand to show that the traditional forms of sculpture and painting condition pictorial versions of the subject more than does any over-conscientious reading of the text, or other learned preoccupation. For the next scene (Fig. 8) the text is unusually laconic, merely stating that Armida had Rinaldo placed in her chariot,[227] so that here, as was not generally the case, it imposed no conditions on the painter, who had carte blanche to do as he pleased. The composition chosen by the French artist Simon Vouet for a painting that is one of a series of twelve devoted to the story of Rinaldo and Armida, was executed in 1630, a few years after his return to Paris from a long Italian sojourn.[228] In the manner in which the female figure at the left leans backward as she supports the sleeping Rinaldo, and in the relation of Rinaldo's head to the upthrust right shoulder with its drooping arm, it recalls the similarly disposed figures in Raphael's *Entombment* (Fig. 9); and it may have been equally suggested to Vouet by some Italian illustration of Tasso's subject like the animated version in Stockholm attributed to Pietro da Cortona (Fig.10),[229] where Armida appears aboard her chariot which is equipped with an extra pair of horses. It will be noted, however, that supporting Rinaldo's legs in the picture by Vouet are two putti not present in the Da Cortona; and one may compare with the Vouet in this regard an engraving of a painting by Poussin (Fig. 11) which displays in the center the sleeping Rinaldo supported now by one female figure instead of two, and by a considerable group of putti.[230] And this interesting version of Poussin may be compared in turn with a fragment of an antique sarcophagus (Fig. 4) visible in Rome in the seventeenth century, representing a parody perhaps, with putti for actors, of the pathetic theme of the dying Meleager's last homecoming,[231] where one will observe a putto supporting the legs of the dying figure in a manner similar to that employed by the putti in the paintings of Poussin and Vouet. It may also be compared with the central part of a drawing of Michelangelo (Fig. 12) where a group of putti, several in attitudes not dissimilar to those in Poussin's picture, are carrying the carcass of a dead deer.[232] It is quite obvious then, that the composition employed by Vouet and Poussin for this episode from the *Gerusalemme liberata* is an entombment composition that has its origins in antiquity. It was available to these artists in several versions besides the parody noted above, as it had been in the sixteenth century to Raphael and to Michelangelo, who in turn may have given suggestions to the seventeenth-century painters.[233] As for Poussin's picture, it is further interesting to observe that the left-hand group of the river god and attendant nymphs was certainly suggested by the group at the right in Marcantonio's engraving after Raphael's drawing of the *Judgment of Paris* (Fig. 13).[234]

The following moment in the story is the transportation of Rinaldo through the air to

227. Canto XIV, stanza 68. The "lente ma tenacissime catene" of flowers with which she had bound him is generally visible in paintings of this subject.

228. For a description of this entire series of paintings, see L. Demonts, "Les amours de Renaud et d'Armide," *Bulletin de la société de l'histoire de l'art français*, VII, 1913, 58–78. I am very much indebted to M. de Villeneuve for his courteous permission to have the paintings photographed.

229. See Catalogue of 1928, no. 27.

230. According to Grautoff (*op. cit.*, II, p. 261) this engraving by Massé is of a lost picture. It corresponds, how-ever, very exactly to a drawing in the Louvre. For a similar version in a private collection, see Friedlaender, *op. cit.*, p. 115; illustration p. 180.

231. It was set into the wall of the Villa Borghese built in 1615. See Robert, *op. cit.*, III, Part 2, p. 358; pl. XCVIII, fig. 307.

232. See K. Frey, *Die Handzeichnungen Michelangelos*, Berlin, 1911, III, pp. 89–91.

233. See Robert, *op. cit.*, III, Part 2, p. 343; pl. XCIV, fig. 283; *ibid.*, II, 64; pl. XXIV, fig. 57.

234. Professor Panofsky called my attention to this resemblance.

Armida's miraculous pleasure dome in the Fortunate Isles.[235] This occurs very rarely in painting and like the preceding scene was never prominent in the Italian illustrated editions. Now in the preceding scene, as we have observed, Armida and a female attendant convey Rinaldo to a chariot drawn by horses, and where the scene occurs in the illustrated editions it is horses that draw the chariot through the air.[236] But in Guercino's fresco in the Palazzo Costaguti at Rome (Fig. 14) one is surprised to find the chariot no longer drawn by horses but by dragons, which nowhere appear in the text of the *Gerusalemme liberata*. Their presence is, however, easily explained by the fact that the painter, casting about in his repertory of pictorial motives for one that would assist him in depicting this event in the story of Rinaldo and Armida, found the appropriate model in some antique representation of the final event in the Medea of Euripides, where Medea transports through the air the dead bodies of her children, whom she has slain to be avenged on Jason, in a chariot drawn by winged dragons. One may see this moment represented in a drawing of a lost fragment of an antique sarcophagus (Fig. 15).[237] It is equally if not more probable, however, that Guercino saw a woodcut of the event as described by Ovid, where Medea after setting fire to Jason's palace and slaying their children, who lie dismembered upon the ground, escapes through the air alone. Such an illustration of the scene (Fig. 16) appears in an abbreviated edition of the *Metamorphoses* containing many woodcuts that was first published at Lyons in 1557,[238] and in general established the type of illustration in other editions in many parts of Europe. Thus just as the witch Armida driving her chariot through the air had her antique forbear in Tasso's mind in the witch Medea driving her chariot of dragons, so Guercino found in some antique or modern illustration of the Medea story the appropriate pictorial material that he required.

The fifteenth canto tells of the voyage of the Christian warriors Carlo and Ubaldo to seek Rinaldo in the Fortunate Isles. Having arrived in the domain of Armida, they ascend the hill that is crowned by her palace, making their way with difficulty through various perils. And the last of these is the grave temptation to love and loiter prepared for them in the song of the nymphs who disport themselves in a pool, while a banquet sumptuously spread on a nearby table invites them to dine.[239] I have discovered no example of this scene among Italian painters, but the Italianate Vouet of necessity included it in his extensive illustration, already mentioned, of the story of Rinaldo and Armida (Fig. 17). The moment is that when the warriors state their emphatic refusal to be tempted by the blandishments of the nymphs, whom they treat as ungallantly and as firmly as Odysseus treated Circe on a similar occasion. Now the composition of Vouet's picture shows scant respect for the poetic text, which describes the bathing place of the nymphs as a lake formed by the sudden widening of a small river that ran through Armida's verdant meadows.[240] And had Vouet consulted the handsome edition of the *Gerusalemme liberata* published in 1617 with en-

235. Canto xiv, stanza 68.

236. In the Venice editions of 1611 and 1625 the main event in the illustration for Canto xiv is Godfrey's dream, but Armida appears driving Rinaldo in her chariot high in the air and in the distance.

237. See Robert, ii, 205; pl. lxii, fig. 193. The dragons are not in Euripides either, but were supplied by the scholiast.

238. The woodcuts are by Bernard Salomon. The illustrations in figs. 16 and 23 are from pp. 89 and 132 of a similar edition in Italian published at Lyons in 1559 (see A. Cartier, *Bibliographie des éditions des De Tournes*, Paris, 1937, i, 15; ii, 450, 500). Mr. Philip Hofer called my attention to these editions and to the Ovid of 1619 (see note

241), and kindly allowed me to have illustrations made from his copies.

239. Stanzas 56–66. See especially 58:
   "Quivi di cibi preziosa e cara
   Apprestata è una mensa in su le rive;
   E scherzando sen van per l'acqua chiara
   Due donzellette garrule e lascive,
   Ch'or si spruzzano il volto, or fanno a gara
   Chi prima a un segno destinato arrive.
   Si tuffano talora, e il capo e il dorso
   Scoprono alfin dopo il celato corso."

240. Stanza 57:
   "Così n'andâr sin dove il fiume vago
   Si spande in maggior letto, e forma un lago."

gravings by the Genoese Bernardo Castello, he might have seen a composition reasonably close to Tasso's description (Fig. 19). For in the illustration to the fifteenth canto we actually see the nymphs disporting themselves in what one might call a small lake beside which stand the warriors in maneristic attitudes typical of Castello's style, while behind is the "tondo edificio" of Armida's palace, and in the extreme foreground the Goddess Fortuna who awaits the outcome of the adventure. But Vouet's composition is, I think, definitely related to that of the Actaeon myth as the latter had been developed by the painters and engravers of the Renaissance. This will be seen if one compares it with an engraving from a French translation of Ovid's *Metamorphoses* published in Paris in 1619 (Fig. 20).[241] In both we have the same essential theme of the discovery of naked loveliness, though with widely different results for the discoverer. And one may note the close compositional similarities that scarcely need enumeration of the bathers in a shallow pool at the right with a buttress or grotto of rock behind from which water pours into the pool either from an opening in the rock or manipulated by a putto, while the protagonist is seen at the left with an opening of space behind him. Vouet might also have seen when he was in Italy Annibale Carracci's version of the subject (Fig. 18), or some other with essentially the same composition; and it is worth noting here again that the earliest prototype of these Baroque compositions is to be found in antiquity. Thus a painting in the House of Sallust in Pompeii (Fig. 21)[242] shows, like Vouet's picture (Fig. 17), the pool and rocky grotto at one side with the water descending on Diana from above—a tradition resurrected in the High Renaissance, to the discredit of the marble basins of the Quattrocento *cassoni* which served as decorative but crowded bathing quarters for Diana and her company.[243]

Having escaped the temptation of Armida's nymphs, the warriors press on through the palace to the enchanted garden modeled after the eternal spring of the gardens of Alcinous in the *Odyssey* with their imperishable fruits and blooms, where from behind thick bushes they descry the Christian Achilles, whose return is essential to the success of the Crusaders, in the lap of his mistress. The passage in the sixteenth canto which describes the beauty of the garden and the langorous passion of the lovers, is one of the most famous in Italian literature, combining as it does in stanzas of superbly musical utterance Tasso's intense sensitiveness to earthly beauty, and his melancholy preoccupation with its untimely decay.[244] That it should be the all-popular subject from Tasso among the Italian and French painters for more than two centuries is easily understood. And here, if anywhere, since the scene was described with elaborate detail, one might expect the painter to follow the admonition of the critics accurately to follow the text. Now in point of fact, Annibale Carracci who probably was the first to paint this subject, and one or two close imitators, were scrupulously accurate. In Carracci's intolerable picture (Fig. 22), which does as much

241. P. 76. Engraving by Isaac Briot II.

242. The illustration is from F. and F. Niccolini, *Le case e monumenti di Pompeii*, vol. III.

243. For illustrations of the Actaeon story in antiquity and the early Renaissance see Biagio Pace, "Metamorfosi figurate," *Bolletino d'arte*, XXVII, 1933–34, pp. 487–507. It may be worth noting that in the sixteenth-century paintings of Titian at Bridgewater House, and of Jacopo Zucchi (see H. Voss, "Jacopo Zucchi," *Zeitschrift für bildende Kunst*, XXIV, 1913, p. 160), the moment of discovery is represented with Actaeon appearing in his normal estate of manhood before transformation has begun; whereas in the more sprightly and naïve but less humanistic painting of the Quattrocento the moment of discovery is combined with transformation, Actaeon being shown with the head

and antlers of a stag. In antiquity (as in the illustration for the Ovid of 1619) Actaeon is regularly a man, as one would expect, but the horns sprouting from his head indicate that transformation has begun. Dr. Kurt Weitzmann has called my attention to a unique representation of Actaeon in a Byzantine manuscript (*Homilies of Gregory Nazianzenus*) of the eleventh century in which he is represented as a huntsman at the left, and at the right is on the ground torn to pieces by dogs, with his human head and body still left, but with the forelegs and hindlegs of a stag (see MS. Jerusalem, Τάφου 14, fol. 308 r., discussed in Athanaios Papadopoulos Kerameus, *Catalogue of the Greek Manuscripts of the Patriarchal Library in Jerusalem*, I, 62).

244. Stanzas 1–17.

violence to the sentiment of the poem as it faithfully reproduces its detail, one can discover the flowers, birds, grapes and the like that Tasso describes, and can note as well the accurate manner in which Rinaldo holds the mirror into which Armida gazes as she braids her tresses, while he himself gazing upward finds his own mirror in her eyes.[245] The positions of the two figures are also suggested by the text, although it is worth noting that the group very closely resembles the Venus and Adonis in the illustrated Ovid, already mentioned, of 1557 (Fig. 23),[246] and in subsequent editions deriving therefrom. The arrangement of figures in the two groups is, in fact, almost identical, closer indeed than are Carracci's Rinaldo and Armida to the lovers as Castello represented them in his uninspired engraving for the sixteenth canto in the first illustrated edition of the *Gerusalemme* published in Genoa in 1590, where, however, the grouping is not essentially different (Fig. 24). But Carracci's dull accuracy of rendering was soon dispensed with in the interest of a more significant interpretation of the episode. Not long after 1630 the Neapolitan artist Paolo Finoglio painted a brilliantly decorative series of pictures illustrating the *Gerusalemme liberata*, four of which were devoted to the story of Rinaldo and Armida.[247] In the painting of the garden episode (Fig. 25) one observes a dramatically pictorial treatment in light and shade that is appropriate to the moment of discovery and to the expression of the lovers' dreamy yet intense passion which the artist has been at pains to suggest in their facial expressions. Paolo Finoglio evidently read the *Gerusalemme* "con amore," and more than any other artist has preserved in his illustrations the spirit of its romantic sentiment. He has preserved a great deal more of it, for instance, than did Tiepolo, when something over a century later he painted his version of the enchanted garden (Fig. 26),[248] an infinitely finer picture in the large clarity and elegance of its design and in the plastic realization of the figures, but in which the intense sentiment of the Baroque has given way to the arch tenderness of the Rococo. But both artists treat the text of the poem freely in the interest of expressive emphasis or pictorial effect, and although a sixteenth-century critic like Lomazzo or Borghini would have praised Finoglio for his expression of human emotion, he might have taken him to task for placing Rinaldo and Armida in the open country instead of in the garden enclosed by the circular palace as Tasso specified, just as he might have objected to Tiepolo's drastic rearrangement of Tasso's architecture and landscape. Certainly the stickler for literary accuracy would have commented on the manner in which Paolo Finoglio in the following scene representing Rinaldo's departure from Armida (Fig. 27), has introduced two figures who have no part in Tasso's narrative: the figure in the left foreground who is helping to launch the boat and the boatman with the oar, both of whom however—and this is the point—are essential elements of this striking Baroque composition.

---

245. Stanzas 18–23:

"Sovra lui pende; ed ei nel grembo molle
Le posa il capo, e il volto al volto attolle;

* * * * *

Dal fianco de l'amante, estranio arnese,
Un cristallo pendea lucido e netto.
Sorse, e quel fra le mani a lui sospese,
Ai misteri d'Amor ministro eletto:
Con luci ella ridenti, ei con accese,
Mirano in vari oggetti un solo oggetto;
Ella del vetro a sè fa specchio, ed egli
Gli occhi di lei sereni a sè fa spegli.

* * * * *

Poi che intrecciò le chiome e che ripresse
Con ordin vago i lor lascivi errori,

Torse in anella i crin minuti, e in esse,
Quasi smalto su l'ôr, consparse i fiori."

This last detail Carracci has omitted.

246. See note 238.

247. See Mario d'Orsi, "Paolo Finoglio, pittore napoletano," *Iapigia* (*Organo della R. Deputazione di Storia Patria per le Puglie*), XVII, 1938, 358 ff.

248. Reproduced through the courtesy of the Art Institute of Chicago. This is one of a brilliant series of four paintings by Tiepolo in the Institute dealing with the Rinaldo-Armida story. Another series of four—in fresco—are in the Villa Valmarama near Vicenza. Two fine Tiepolos depicting the same story—one of the garden scene—are in the Alte Pinakothek in Munich. What appears to be a sketch for the latter is in the Kaiser-Friedrich Museum in Berlin.

For this last scene of Rinaldo's departure, there were also versions more faithful to the text; and in the case of Poussin's fine drawing in the Louvre (Fig. 28) this might seem at first to be sufficiently explained by the artist's respect for the dramatic and scenic essentials of the story and his unwillingness to introduce foreign material that might, like Finoglio's boatman, make for an effective composition per se, but not for one that could be said to emphasize the dramatic relationship between Rinaldo and Armida. But here, as in his illustration of the first episode of the story (Fig. 1) where Poussin, as we have seen, adopted motives from the Endymion sarcophagi for a scene similar in content, antiquity lent a strong, guiding hand. For in antique representations of Theseus abandoning the sleeping Ariadne on the island of Naxos—in the fine example, for instance, in the House of the Tragic Poet in Pompeii (Fig. 29)[249]—a subject that had in common with Tasso's the half-reluctant desertion of a former mistress who lies unconscious on the seashore (Armida in contrast to Ariadne is not sleeping, but has swooned), Poussin found a composition that was almost made to order for his illustration of Tasso.

If we compare his drawing with the ancient painting, we see in the left foreground of both the unconscious female figure in the classical attitude of sleep with a rocky eminence behind; and at the right the sea with the departing lover who turns to his mistress with a look of sorrowful farewell as he is helped or hurried, as the case may be, into the waiting boat. Tasso's text required the mountain in the background which, in a general way, parallels the rocky hill in the Pompeian painting; it also required the two warriors with whom we are already familiar who urge Rinaldo into the boat. The curve of the boat resembling the curve in the ancient fresco may be seen barely indicated at the extreme right, while the goddess Fortuna, whose body is half cut off by the frame, sits in the boat (as she actually does in a number of book illustrations that Poussin certainly knew) stretching out an arm to the three who are about to disembark. It will be noted that Poussin's alteration, such as it is, of the antique composition is characteristically in the interest of greater pictorial unity that makes for dramatic concentration. The mountain's powerful pyramid almost encloses both groups of figures within its contours, enforcing their dramatic relationship, and the boat at the right in contrast to its more complete depiction in the ancient painting (including the realistic detail of unfurling the "perjured sails") is barely suggested, as if Poussin, though willing in the interest of clear illustration to indicate the means of departure, had refused to permit any picturesque intrusion on the concentrated human drama of farewell.

It is probable that Tasso had the abandonment of Ariadne in mind when he wrote the conclusion to Rinaldo's infatuation for Armida; it is certain that he had in mind another famous desertion of antiquity—Aeneas' desertion of Dido in Carthage; for Armida, before she swoons, curses Rinaldo in the identical language of Dido's famous curse uttered during her final moments with Aeneas. In any event, for this episode the ancient world provided both painter and poet with absolutely parallel source material which they recreated to produce forms that were strikingly analogous to their prototypes, the antique language suffering less alteration here than in any scene hitherto considered.

Poussin, of course, never saw the painting in Pompeii, but it would seem virtually certain that he had seen in Rome a similar pictorial rendering of what was long a popular subject in Roman art. Or he could certainly have seen a relief like that reported to have been excavated at Hadrian's villa in the sixteenth century (Fig. 30),[250] which itself contains most

---

249. For the Greek ancestry of this composition and of that in Fig. 28 see G. E. Rizzo, *La pittura ellenistico-romana*, Milan, 1929, p. 25.

250. See W. Helbig, *Führer durch die öffentlichen Sammlungen klassischer Altertümer in Rom*, 3rd ed., Leipzig, 1912, p. 138. Poussin's interest in the story of Bacchus and

of the chief elements in his composition, and could in the absence of a painting have served as its prototype. An interesting variant on Poussin's drawing is found in Vouet's painting in Paris (Fig. 31) with its obvious shift of background elements to place the sea behind Ariadne and the boat before the rocky cliff. The entire boat appears here, though dominated as an element in the composition by the figures, just as it is in the panoramic engraving of Antonio Tempesta (Fig. 32) executed before 1630, and probably during the period of Vouet's Italian sojourn,[251] which certainly provided the French painter with his immediate model. But probably for Tempesta, as certainly for Poussin, the immediate model was the antique.

It is hoped that enough evidence has been produced to show that the learned painter is, in the sense in which the Renaissance and Baroque critics frequently conceived him, something of a myth. This unreal conception, an inevitable accretion in the often pedantic criticism of the middle and late sixteenth century, of the theory of the sister arts—a theory which is significant only if unburdened of the supercargo of great erudition—must indeed share the responsibility for much unmemorable painting produced by the French and other academies in the course of their history. But fortunately it could have little or no serious influence on the significant practice and development of the art. What the critics in effect urged the painter to do was to read his text carefully, and then, in an accurate pictorial transcription, give a full account of his literary stewardship. What the painter actually did, has been the subject of this chapter.

VIII—VIRTÙ VISIVA

It will be remembered that Leonardo blamed the poet for possessing that manifold learning which the doctrine *ut pictura poesis* sought to thrust upon the painter, and for that reason considered him little more than a monger of the intellectual wares of other men.[252] This opinion of poetry, and others equally derogatory that appear in the celebrated *paragone*, no fair-minded critic will, of course, approve; and perhaps they represent some distortion of Leonardo's real opinion. For in the *paragone* he appears not only as the sincere and ardent champion of the art of painting, but also as one holding a kind of imaginary debate with a defender of poetry, as he might actually have done at the court of the Sforzas, and arguing perhaps with lively exaggeration to get the better of his opponent.[253] The traditional elements, or some of them at least, that appear in his defense of painting Leonardo probably includes less from conviction than to serve the purpose of his argument: such he could have adopted from Pliny or Alberti or learned from his contemporaries, for they were the current jargon of the age. Thus he argues that if invention belongs to the poet's art,

Ariadne is further shown by two drawings in Windsor (nos. 11888ᵛ and 11911) that Professors Panofsky and Friedlaender have called to my attention. Though the compositions are different, both drawings appear to represent Bacchus accompanied by his usual attendants standing before Ariadne, who is seated next to another woman who appears to console her or to persuade her to regard Bacchus with favor. The figure of the woman does not occur in classical art in Bacchus-Ariadne compositions. Problems concerning classical prototypes raised by these drawings cannot be discussed here. I mention the drawings only as further evidence of Poussin's interest in this story (cf. his *Bacchanal* in Madrid in which Ariadne appears with Bacchus), since an ancient illustration of one of its episodes

provided him with his composition for the *Abandonment of Armida*. No. 11911 is reproduced in *Old Master Drawings*, III, 1928–29, p. 16.

251. Tempesta lived and worked in Rome most of his life. He died in 1630.

252. *Trattato*, I, 23: "Che nessuna di queste cose, di che egli parla, è sua professione propria, ma che, s'ei vol' parlare et orare, è da persuadere, che in questo egli è vinto dall' oratore; e se parla di Astrologia, che lo ha rubato all' astrologo, e di filosofia, al filosofo, e che in effetto la poesia non ha propria sedia, nè la merita altramente, che di un merciajo ragunatore di mercanzie fatte da diversi artigiani."

253. See Richter, *The Literary Works of Leonardo da Vinci*, pp. 41 ff.

so does it also to the painter's;[254] if poetry can teach, so too can painting;[255] the vivid reality of the painter's images leads lovers to converse with portraits of their beloved, or incites men to worship as poetry cannot; and when it comes to deception the painter is supreme, and Leonardo avows to have seen a monkey indulging in endless pranks when he saw another monkey represented in a picture.[256] Likewise one must discount as pardonable hyperbole or simply set down as bad aesthetic most of Leonardo's original comparisons of painting with poetry, to the latter's grievous disadvantage. He argues for instance that the sense of sight to which painting appeals is nobler than the sense of hearing to which poetry appeals,[257] or that the darkness of the mind's eye in which poetry is born, in short the poetic imagination, is inferior to the bodily eye of the painter which directly apprehends the rich and wonderful variety of the external world as the inner eye of the poet cannot.[258] In fact the sum of his argument is to deny nearly all reality to the poet's creations, simply because the medium of his art makes no direct impact on the organ of vision. But granting the presence of some matter that is merely conventional and of much that is aesthetically specious (however lively and original), the *paragone* still contains some very shrewd criticism. And if we survey the monotonous unanimity of the critics concerning the blessed sisterhood of poetry and painting, it is at least refreshing to find one who had the independent conviction to maintain that far from being identical twins, they were in important respects totally different. And of the differences noted by Leonardo one is fundamental and was to play an important part in the later history of criticism.

When Leonardo is explaining why the painter's depiction of a battle is superior to the poet's—a superiority that he measures in terms of directness, vividness, and truth—he declares that in contrast to the long and tedious description of a poem, the painter shows the vivid and manifold action of a battle in a single instant;[259] and he says much the same thing when he comments on the poet's disadvantage as compared with the painter in the representation of bodily beauty. Thus the poet must render things piecemeal as "if a face were to be revealed bit by bit, with the part previously shown covered up, so that we are prevented by our own forgetfulness from comparing any harmony of proportions, because the eye cannot embrace the whole simultaneously in its field of vision," whereas a painting would represent all the parts of the face at the same instant, like so many voices joined together in sweet harmony.[260] This passage recalls Lessing's famous comment on the indistinctness of Ariosto's long and detailed description of Alcina which Dolce, as we have seen, praised as a model for painters to follow[261]—a comment in which Lessing illustrates his view that since the successive addition of details in description cannot result in a clear

254. *Trattato*, I, 25.

255. *Ibid.*, 21: "Per l'una e per l'altra si può dimostrare molti morali costumi, come fece Apelle co' la sua calunnia." Cf. 19 for a similar reference to Apelles.

256. For all these instances of the efficacy of painting see *ibid.*, 14.

257. *Ibid.*: "La pittura serve à più degno senso, che la poesia, e fa con più verità le figure delle opere di natura che il poeta."

258. *Ibid.*, 15: "Si ritrova la poesia nella mente ovvero immaginativa del poeta, il quale finge le medesime cose del pittore, per le quali fintioni egli vole equipararsi a esso pittore, ma invero ei n'è molto rimoto . . . Adonque in tal caso di fintione diremo con verità esser tal proportione della scientia della pittura alla poesia, qual è dal corpo alla sua ombra derivativa, et ancora maggior proportione, conciosiacche l'ombra di tal corpo almeno entra per l'occhio al senso comune, ma la immaginatione di tal corpo non entra in esso senso, ma li nasce, nell' occhio tenebroso. O,

che differentia è à immaginare tal luce nel l'occhio tenebroso al vederla in atto fuori delle tenebre."

259. *Ibid.*: "Se tu, poeta, figurerai la sanguinosa battaglia, si sta con la oscura e tenebrosa aria, mediante il fumo delle spaventevoli et mortali machine, mista co' la spessa polvere intorbidatrice dell' aria, e la paurosa fuga de-li miseri spaventati dalla orribile morte? In questo caso il pittore ti supera, perchè la tua penna fia consumata, innanzi che tu descriva appieno quel, che immediate il pittore ti rappresenta co' la sua scientia. E la tua lingua sarà impedita dalla sete, e il corpo dal sonno e fame, prima chè tu co' parole dimostri quello, che in un istante il pittore ti dimostra . . . lunga e tediosissima cosa sarebbe alla poesia a ridire tutti li movimenti de li operatori di tal guerra, e le parti delle membra, e lor' ornamenti, delle quali cose la pittura finita con gran' brevità e verità ti pone innanzi."

260. *Ibid.*, 21. The translation is from Richter, *op. cit.* p. 60.

261. See p. 4 and notes 10 and 11.

and definite image of coexistent forms, descriptive poetry is not the province of the poet, and cannot challenge painting in depicting the beauty of the external world. And in pointing out the painter's capacity, which the poet does not share, to represent figures or details that one apprehends in a single moment of time, Leonardo clearly anticipates Lessing's virtually identical definition of painting as an art of figures coexistent in space that has for its province the depiction of objective reality.[262] Furthermore when he observes that "the only true office of the poet is to invent the words of people, who are conversing together,"[263] he seems to have in mind something that approximates Lessing's definition of poetry as an art of words succeeding one another in time in which, as the German critic was to add, the poet must deal not with description, but with progressive human actions and emotions.[264] Leonardo thus anticipated by two and a half centuries Lessing's famous distinction between poetry and painting.

Now it is self-evident, despite the abstract logic of cubism or the vagaries of expressionism, that the painter's art must generally be based on the representation of the natural world as apprehended by the eye, and the fact that major provinces of the painter's art— landscape, interior scenes, and still-life—represent definite categories of visual experience that have no analogies among the historical genres of literature, is eloquent illustration of this truth.[265] It does not follow, however, as Leonardo argued, that painting is the superior art, or even that its images of the world of nature are more vivid, for who can say that "that inward eye which is the bliss of solitude" of which the poet wrote presents less vivid images to the mind than the natural eye. In the early eighteenth century when we begin to see in literature the first stirrings of an interest in the beauty of external nature that was to culminate in the Romantic Movement, a critic of literature, Joseph Addison, again praised the sense of sight in words that would have won high praise from Leonardo himself: "Our sight," he says, "is the most perfect and most delightful of all our senses. It fills the mind with the largest variety of ideas, converses with its objects at the greatest distance, and continues the longest in action without being tired or satiated with its proper enjoyments."[266] And when the English man of letters writes that "description runs yet further from the things it represents than painting; for a picture bears a real resemblance to its original which letters and syllables are wholly void of,"[267] he seems merely to echo at a distance of two centuries Leonardo's famous remark that painting stands to poetry in the same relation as a body to its cast shadow, since "poetry puts down her subjects in imaginary written characters, while painting puts down the identical reflections that the eye receives as if they were real."[268] Addison goes on to say that "colors speak all languages, but words are understood only by such a people or nation,"[269] an observation that he probably owed to De Piles,[270] but which again may trace its ancestry in the Renaissance to Leonardo's remark that lit-

262. *Laokoön* xvi–xx.

263. *Trattato*, I, 15: "Solo il vero uffitio del poeta è fingere parole di gente, che insieme parlino, e sol' queste rappresenta al senso dell' audito tanto, come naturali, perchè in se sono naturali create dall' humana voce. Et in tutte l'altre consequentie è superato dal pittore." But Leonardo later remarks that to imitate in words the actions and speeches of men is less noble than to imitate the God-created works of nature whereby painters become "nipoti à Dio" (*ibid.*, 14 and 19). And in another passage Leonardo says that it is the visual imagery of description of the beauties of nature—that part of his art in which he must be surpassed by the painter—that reflects honor on the poet (*ibid.*, 20).

264. *Loc. cit.*

265. "Descriptive poetry" is a term that suggests a kind

of poetry analogous in a general way to landscape, still-life' etc. in painting, but it was precisely the "Schilderungs-sucht" in modern poetry that Lessing attacked and with great good reason. The historical genres of literature— tragedy, comedy, epic, lyric, satire, etc.—are so named chiefly for the type of human content each has to express.

266. *Spectator*, No. 411 (June 21, 1712).

267. *Ibid.*, No. 416 (June 27).

268. *Op. cit.*, I, 2; the translation from Richter, p. 52.

269. *Spectator*, No. 416.

270. See Dryden's translation of his commentary on Du Fresnoy, p. 83: "The Advantage which Painting possesses above Poesie is this; that amongst so great a Diversity of Languages, she makes her self understood by all the Nations of the World."

erature requires commentators and explanations, whereas the work of a painter (since, Leonardo means, his language is the universal language of sight) will be understood by all who behold it.[271] And this was a notion that in later criticism was curiously inconsistent with the doctrine of the learned painter, for whereas the one praised the language of painting as superior to that of poetry in its universal appeal, the other sought to turn this language into a mere pictorial equivalent of literary texts, in short to make it a language that none but the initiate could understand. But when Addison comes to write of what he calls the secondary pleasures of the imagination—those that do not result directly from the sight of natural objects, but may accompany the experience of works of art or literature—he speaks of the power of words to evoke vivid images in the mind's eye in a way that is directly opposed to the doctrine of Leonardo, and contains a truth of which the Florentine was scarcely aware. For if painting reproduces nature with an objective reality that words can never attain (so far he would agree with Leonardo), still "words, when well chosen, have so great a force in them that a description often gives us more lively ideas than a sight of things themselves."[272] The inward eye thus possesses for the literary critic at least as keen a sight as the outward eye possessed for the critic of painting, but with this point of view the Abbé du Bos, whose thinking along these lines was thoroughly Leonardesque, was a few years later to disagree. Du Bos makes a distinction that recalls Leonardo between the "signes naturels" of painting and the "signes artificiels" of poetry,[273] and argues that the former act more powerfully on the human imagination than the latter because they act, as Leonardo would have said, "per la via della virtù visiva"—through the power of sight.[274] And so it follows for Du Bos that the most moving poetry is tragedy, not only for its expressive power, but because it resembles painting to the extent that it is a spectacle presented on the stage and so appeals directly to the eye.[275]

It is unprofitable to argue, as Leonardo did, that the mind's eye sees more darkly than the outward eye or that the poet's imagery leaves less vivid marks on the mind than the painter's conveys to the sight, for on the basis of their own experience some will always agree with Leonardo, others with Addison. But it would certainly be the consensus of opinion that if descriptive poetry or prose produces a series of vivid images in the mind, these do not, in general experience, unite to form a clear simultaneous impression of various forms, details, and colors, such as one has in beholding a picture or a scene in nature. But the point which should be made here is that at the beginning of the eighteenth century a new impulse to seek the beginnings of knowledge not in any a priori endowment of the human soul, but in the data of sense experience, led to a new awareness of the senses as organs of knowledge. And between Leonardo, greatest exemplar of the empirical ardor of the Renaissance, at the beginning of the sixteenth century, and Du Bos near the beginning of the eighteenth, the clear insistence that painting is primarily an art whose function it is to represent to the eye the forms and beauty of the external world was in eclipse.[276] It was in eclipse, that is, during the two centuries in which the doctrine *ut pictura poesis* was in process of

271. *Op. cit.*, 22: "Et anchorche le cose de' poeti sieno con lungo intervallo di tempo lette, spesse sono le volte, chelle non sono intese e bisogna farli sopra diversi comenti ... Ma l'opera del pittore immediate è compresa dalli suoi riguardatori." Elsewhere (19) Leonardo says that the poet's names are not universal like the painter's forms. Armenini (*De' veri precetti della pittura*, 1, 3, p. 33) remarks in like manner that poetry requires study, time, and doctrine (here speaks the Counter-Reform), but that painting is apprehended immediately by every rank and type of person.

272. *Loc. cit.*

273. *Réflexions critiques*, 1, 40, pp. 415 ff.

274. *Ibid.*; cf. Leonardo, *op. cit.*, 1, 2.

275. *Ibid.*, p. 425; cf. 1, 13, pp. 105 ff., and Horace *Ars poetica* 180 ff.

276. The occasional compliments to painting as speaking a more universal language than poetry were stock in trade and do not alter the truth of this statement. See notes 270 and 271.

evolution, when the critics were all too eager to turn the poet into a painter of pictures and the painter into one who shared subject matter and expression and a set of rules for good invention with the poet. And it was in the writing of Du Bos, who was deeply influenced by the empiricism of the English philosopher John Locke and by Addison's essays (themselves owing much to Locke) on the effect of visual experience on the imagination,[277] that we first find in the criticism of painting any well-formulated theory that is opposed to the abstract doctrine of the Academicians. For in applying the rules of poetry to painting, critics like Félibien and Le Brun had so intellectualized the pictorial art that its primary character as a visual art capable of affecting the human imagination only through its initial power over the sense of sight, was largely neglected.

But if painting to Leonardo could more vividly than poetry represent the beauty of a face, or of forests, valleys, fields, and streams,[278] it could also—and here Leonardo argues against those who would claim for poetry the total realm of the mind's activity—represent the motions of the mind, by which he chiefly means the passions of the soul in so far as they are expressed by movements of the body.[279] And when in the *Trattato*, he was not defending painting against poetry and there was no occasion for pressing the argument, Leonardo expressly states, as we have seen, that it is in the manifestation of the mind's activity through bodily movement (not in the depiction of the beauty of nature of which he sometimes writes with so much personal feeling and imagination)[280] that the most important part of the painter's art lies.[281] Thus in arguing that the province of the mind is not denied to the painter, Leonardo at the same time restricts him to that inward activity that through the body makes itself palpable to the sight. And this again was an excellent distinction and one that later critics who tended to read into painting more expression of the thinking and feeling man than the painter could possibly depict in a single figure would have done well to consider. The implications of Leonardo's distinction are brought out in the mid-sixteenth century, when Dolce describes the painter as one intent on imitating through lines and colors all that is represented to the eye—and this, of course, includes the depiction of mental and of psychic life through expressive bodily movement—and the poet as imitating with words not only the external world (wherein most critics considered him a painter) but also "that which is represented to the intellect."[282] By this phrase Dolce would appear to mean intellectual concepts and the temporal processes of thought, as distinguished from visual imagery. A few years earlier, Benedetto Varchi had also maintained this same general distinction, arguing that it is chiefly the poet's business to imitate *il di dentro*—the concepts, and passions of the soul, that are within—and the painter's, *il di fuori*—the bodies and features of the outer world.[283] He added prudently

277. For Du Bos's debt to Locke and Addison see A. Lombard, *L'Abbé du Bos, un initiateur de la pensée moderne*, Paris, 1913, pp. 194 ff.; p. 206; p. 221.

278. *Trattato*, I, 18.

279. *Ibid.*, 19: "Se la poesia s'estende in filosofia morale, e questa in filosofia naturale; se quella descrive le operationi della mente, che considera quella, se la mente opera nei movimenti."

280. *Ibid.*, II, 68; cf. 66.

281. *Ibid.*, 122: "La più importante cosa, che ne' discorsi della pittura trovare si possa, sono li movimenti appropriati alli accidenti mentali di ciascun animale, come desiderio, sprezzamento, ira, pietà e simili." Cf. III, 297, 368.

282. See note 6.

283. *Due lezzioni*, 1549, pp. 113–14: "I Poeti imitano il di dentro principalmente, cio è i concetti, e le passioni dell' animo, se bene molte volte discrivono ancora, e quasi

dipingono colle parole i corpi, e tutte le fattezze di tutte le cose così animate, come inanimate [in all of this "painting" of the external world Leonardo would have said that the poet cannot successfully rival the painter], et i Pittori imitano principalmente il di fuori, cio è i corpi, e le fattezze di tutte le cose . . . pare che sia tanta differenza fra la Poesia, e la pittura quanta è fra l'anima, e'l corpo [cf. the saying of Leonardo, who favors painting and the natural world, that painting is to poetry as a body to its cast shadow], bene è vero, che come i Poeti discrivono anchora il di fuori, così i Pittori mostrano quanto più possono il di dentro, cio è gl'affetti, et il primo, che cio anticamente facesse questo, secondo che racconta Plinio, fu Aristide Thebano, e modernamente Giotto. Bene è vero, che i Pittori non possono sprimere così felicemente il di dentro, come il di fuori." A similar distinction appears again near the end of the century (1591) in Comanini's differentiation

that they may invade each other's territory to some extent, for the poet will also paint, as it were, the outer world, and the painter will represent the "affetti" as best he can, though he can never do this as happily as the poet—a point of view which is again a direct anticipation of the central doctrine of Lessing. But this vital distinction between the sister arts was obscured, if not altogether lost, in the late sixteenth century in the Mannerist doctrine that the painter's standard of artistic imitation was not to be found in selecting the best from external nature, but in contemplating an Idea of perfection—or what Zuccari was to call *disegno interno*—in the mind's eye.[284] And it was not a distinction which, in the seventeenth century, the Cartesian habit of making painting purely a function of the human reason would tend to encourage. Again it was Du Bos in the early eighteenth century who in a discerning chapter on the subjects most suited to the poet and to the painter,[285] distinguished carefully for the first time in nearly two centuries between the painter's field as *di fuori* and the poet's as *di dentro*. Du Bos remarks particularly on the ability of the former to represent, as the poet cannot without loss of unity, the different emotions of a large group of persons simultaneously interested in an action, as well as the age, sex, and dress of each, their individual characters so far as these may be rendered in visible signs, and the setting in which the group is placed, much of which the poet, because his is a temporal art, could only do—and here Leonardo would have again agreed—at the risk of lengthy and tiresome description. But the advantages of the temporal over the spatial art are that the poet can represent the sublime or subtle thought that accompanies the passions of the soul as the painter cannot, for all his greater vividness in portraying the emotions; just as he can render intricacies of moral character denied to the painter, and can impart to events a heightened meaning, because they are dramatically related to preceding events. This last Du Bos calls in the language of his day "le sublime de rapport"—a virtue obviously denied the painter, because he must confine himself to a single event in a single moment of time. In all such arguments one will recognize again, but this time at close range, a direct anticipation of Lessing. But it was Leonardo who, two centuries before, in claiming for the painter the depiction of those aspects of the mind's activity that are revealed in the body, had conceded to the poet other kinds of mental activity that the painter's art is unable to express.[286]

IX—THE UNITY OF ACTION

The preceding parts of this study will, it is hoped, make it clear that antiquity furnished the Renaissance with a body of doctrine intended in particular for dramatic and epic poetry, which the theorists of the sixteenth century cavalierly applied to painting, unaware, to invoke Lessing once more, that there might be difficulties in transferring the criticism of an art of words succeeding one another in time, to an art of figures coexistent in space. Now, in point of fact, sixteenth-century criticism of painting in Italy is singularly free of those anomalies that later arose from the unfortunate attempt to impose correspondences

---

between "imitatione fantastica" as being the chief delight of poetry, and "imitatione icastica" of the painter (see Panofsky, *Idea*, pp. 97–98 for comment on the meaning of these terms). Among literary critics it makes a rare appearance in the later Cinquecento in Castelvetro's virtual restriction of the painter's legitimate activity to the field of realistic portraiture, for in the imitation of ideal nature which is the poet's province the painter, he says, can produce nothing either delightful or of serious merit (*Poetica d'Aristotele vulgarizzata et sposta*, Basel, 1576, pp. 40, 72–73,

586; first ed. 1570). This is obviously to make the distinction in an extreme form and one which does violence to the art of painting.

284. See notes 48 and 108. For discussion of Zuccari's *disegno interno*, see Panofsky, *Idea*, pp. 47 ff.

285. *Op. cit.*, I, 13, pp. 84 ff. See also the excellent chapters on Du Bos's comparison of poetry with painting in Lombard, *op. cit.*, pp. 211–24.

286. See notes 263 and 279. Moral philosophy and human conversation are mentioned specifically as belonging to poetry.

of form rather than of content upon two arts whose primary media were totally different. The theological and dogmatic twist that Gilio da Fabriano in the late sixteenth century gave to the theory of decorum, belonged after all to a different category of criticism, and might be laid at the doors of the theologian and moralist rather than of the critic per se. It was merely an unfortunate extension of the humanistic habit of identifying the content and the high seriousness of poetry and painting, not the result of any consistent attempt of aesthetic criticism to discover relationships of form between the sister arts; and the same might be said of the theory of the learned painter, for only through learning could the painter's productions carry equal weight with poetry and history among scholars and theologians. And the Italian critics of the late sixteenth century, despite their grievous faults of prolixity, unincisiveness, and indiscriminate appropriation of the thought and language of their ancient or immediate predecessors, did not, like some of the more systematic than perceptive exponents of the humanistic theory of painting in seventeenth-century France and England, make the enthusiastic but mistaken attempt to discover, it would seem at any cost, analogies of form between the sister arts.[287] To say, for instance, in the late seventeenth century that the painter like the dramatic poet had observed the unities of place, time, and action was perhaps to pay him as high a compliment as the doctrine *ut pictura poesis* could sponsor,[288] and we have already seen that this particular development of the comparison of painting with poetry was a natural accompaniment of the Cartesian passion for clarity and order.[289]

But the Aristotelian unity of action is not a critical concept which has any real validity for the art of painting. And this will be apparent if we take a moment to consider some further aspects of the discussion reported by Félibien of Poussin's *Fall of the Manna in the Wilderness* (Fig. 1),[290] a painting in which most of the persons represented are watching the falling manna in attitudes of wonder or thanksgiving, or are gathering it up from the ground. A critic of the picture had remarked that Poussin had violated the facts of history when he depicted the manna falling by day, for in reality the Hebrews had found it in the morning spread upon the ground like dew; and that he had also erred when to exemplify the hunger and wretchedness of these people he showed a young woman who suckled her aged mother instead of her child, for according to Scripture the Hebrews had the night before fed on quails which had been sufficient to satisfy their worst hunger (wherefore this episode, the critic means to say, could in reality have taken place only before the quails arrived).[291] To this Le Brun answered that a painter is not like an historian who by a succession of words represents a progressive action; but since he may depict an event as taking place only in a single moment of time, it is sometimes necessary for him to join together many incidents in order that people may understand the subject which he treats. For if he did not do this, they would be no better instructed than if an historian instead of conducting his narrative from beginning to end, contented himself with merely giving the conclusion.[292] Painting then is closely related to the art of story-telling, and Le Brun justifies what he takes to be Poussin's method on didactic grounds, as one might readily expect of a theorist who heartily endorsed the Horatian *monere et delectare*.

287. Cf. p. 8 and notes 26 and 27.
288. It will be recalled that it is only the unity of action that Aristotle insists upon in the *Poetics*. The other unities were first formulated by Castelvetro, who had the highly unimaginative notion that it would be a breach of verisimilitude if the place of the action were not a single spot which changed no more than the stage did, and if the time of the

action did not exactly coincide with the actual time of the performance. Castelvetro was equally unimaginative about the art of painting. See note 283.
289. See p. 30.
290. The date was November 5, 1667.
291. See Jouin, *Conférences*, p. 62.
292. *Ibid.*

We must forego a discussion of Le Brun's ingenious attempt to prove Poussin an accurate historian in the face of this telescoping of events, and proceed to the remarks of another speaker who according to Félibien brought the discussion to a close. For it is here that Aristotle's doctrine of the unity of action is pronounced to be as valid for painting as for dramatic poetry, and that painting is virtually declared to be, like poetry, an art of time. That did not, of course, prevent its being in the eyes of the Academy a spatial art as well, which since it represented a single event at a single moment of time, of necessity observed in pictorial fashion the other dramatic unities—those of time and place. But if this were true, as it obviously was, there was something inconsistent in interpreting Poussin's unity of action in temporal terms.[293]

The Aristotelian theorist begins by observing that if the rules of the theatre allow poets to join together several events that happened at different times in order to make a single action of them, provided there be no inconsistency and that probability ("vraisemblance") be strictly observed, it is yet more right that the painter should have the same freedom, for without it—and the present speaker, it will be noted, bases his argument on aesthetic, not on didactic grounds as had Le Brun—his compositions would be less admirable and his genius displayed to less advantage. Now in this regard, continues the theorist, one cannot accuse Poussin of having put in his painting anything that might impede the unity of action, or anything that is counter to probability or, for that matter, too far removed from historical truth. For if he did not entirely follow the text of Scripture, he could have found the main elements of his story in the *Antiquitates Judaeorum* of Josephus, who relates that after the Jews had received the quails, Moses lifting up his hands prayed God to send them other nourishment, whereupon the manna fell from heaven like drops of dew which grew larger as they descended and which the people took for snow until they had tasted thereof.[294]

Here, at least, was a highly respectable text that, even if it did not have the infallibility of Scripture, might guard Poussin's reputation as an historian; and the speaker now proceeds to develop the idea of the unity of action, remarking that "as for having represented persons some of whom are in misery whereas others are receiving relief, it is here that this learned painter has shown that he is a true poet, for he has composed his work according to the rules which the art of poetry requires one to observe in composing plays for the theatre. For to represent his story perfectly he needed those parts that are necessary to a poem in order to pass from ill to good fortune. That is why we see that the groups of figures whose actions are different are like so many episodes that serve for what one calls *peripateia*, and as a means to make known the changes that came upon the Israelites when they emerged from their extreme wretchedness, and entered into a happier state. Thus their misfortune is represented by people who are languishing and beaten down; the change in their fortune is depicted by the fall of the manna, and their happiness may be seen in their possession of a food that we see them gathering with unbounded joy."[295]

293. See *ibid.*, p. 154, for the interesting remarks of Henri Testelin on the fundamental difference, later emphasized by Lessing, between poetry and painting, and on the unities as they apply to painting (from his lecture on "L'expression générale et particulière"): "Il fut représenté que par l'écriture l'on peut bien faire une ample description de toutes les circonstances qui arrivent en une suite de temps, lesquelles on ne peut concevoir que successivement, mais qu'en la peinture l'on doit comprendre tout d'un coup l'idée du sujet; qu'ainsi un peintre se doit restreindre à ces trois unités, à savoir: ce qui arrive en un seul temps; ce que la vue peut découvrir d'une seule œillade; et ce qui se peut représenter dans l'espace d'un tableau." The first of these unities corresponds to the dramatic unity of time, the second and third together to the dramatic unity of place. It will be noted that none of the three corresponds to Aristotle's unity of action, and quite rightly, because in a spatial art the latter is subsumed in the other two unities. For what can be seen happening in a single place in a single moment of time is bound to have unity of action in a pictorial sense, if the artist knows how to impart dramatic unity to his composition.

294. *Ibid.*, p. 64.

295. *Ibid.*

This is something new in the doctrine *ut pictura poesis*, for hitherto in our discussion we have seen that if the painter fulfilled the requirements of invention, expression, decorum, and the like, which the doctrine imposed upon him, his art would resemble poetry in content rather than in form, for the painter's disposition of his objects was never supposed to be governed by temporal considerations. But in the case of Aristotle's unity of action we have to do with a formal concept designed for dramatic poetry, which the critics of painting sometimes attempted to apply to an art for which, as we shall see, the unity of action was indeed a legitimate concept, but not in the Aristotelian sense.

Now it is obviously impossible to judge French painting of the seventeenth century fairly unless one understands and respects, however strong his disagreement, the view that the great painter is an edifying teacher, and unless one remembers that at no time in the history of painting did critics assume more completely that good painting gathered its subjects and its content from poetry and history. And one must recall as well that in an age when the painter was acknowledged to be moralist, poet, and historian, it was not unnatural that a learned man looking at a picture should read it like a text, as in fact Poussin, although he never admitted the didactic function of art, had actually advised him to do.[296] Nevertheless it is straining the possibilities of expression further than the medium of painting can bear when Félibien's theorist reads the beginning, middle, and end of a drama, considered as developing in time, into the actions and expressions in Poussin's picture. For granted that one knows its biblical source, as he must if he is to understand and judge it for its human as well as its formal content, what the *Fall of the Manna* tells us is what Poussin the painter, not the unknown theorist of the Academy, meant it to tell us: that here is a group of Israelites, male and female, young and old, who react with various emotions to the fall of the manna if they are aware of it; or if they are not, are so portrayed as to illustrate the state of hunger which the miracle of the manna was intended to relieve. This is in effect what Le Brun pointed out in his earlier discussion of the picture, when he remarked on the way in which the actions and expressions therein all bear on the principal subject,[297] and when he might have legitimately added that in this respect the picture showed unity of action. For the unity of action so understood is based squarely (granted that one has the necessary minimum of biblical knowledge) on what the picture itself reveals, not on the temporal concept of the unity of action as Aristotle applied it to the drama. Yet it is the latter with which Félibien's theorist mistakenly, though with every complimentary intention, credits Poussin when, as an enthusiastic disciple of the doctrine *ut pictura poesis*, he seeks to apply a law indispensable to the writing of good drama to an art in which the unity of action must in the very nature of the medium be governed by spatial, not by temporal considerations. To the dramatist the unity of action is invaluable as a principle of criticism, for it points to a standard of abstemious concentration, and warns against the inclusion of the casual and unrelated in an art in which the succession of events in time must move consistently to an inevitable end. But for painting, once the continuous method had been generally abandoned,[298] it could have, in the Aristotelian sense, no meaning, for the counterpart in painting of Aristotle's unity of action—the representation of an event in such a way that all pictorial elements would be simultaneously functional to the expression of a single dramatic action—

296. See p. 30 and note 123.

297. See pp. 29 ff.

298. Félibien in his *Préface* (p. 313) warns not precisely against this method but against including too many actions in a picture which took place in one time and one locality, remarking that a painter who commits these faults deserves

no less censure than did Euripides, whose *Trojan Women* has been blamed by everyone because it represents three separate actions. For the concept of the continuous method see F. Wickhoff, *Roman Art* (trans. E. Strong), London, 1900, pp. 11 ff.

could of necessity (such was the requirement of the medium) include only a single moment of time. Once this is understood, it becomes clear that any attempt to apply to painting the principle of the unity of action in the manner in which Aristotle applied it to the drama, is aesthetically fallacious. And this tendency to think of painting in the temporal terms of literary art leads not only in Félibien's time but sometimes to an appalling degree among later critics of art to the bad habit of finding in their favorite works, "what," as Reynolds observed, "they are resolved to find," as an example of which one might cite Le Brun's psychological analysis of the mingled feelings of the woman in the *Fall of the Manna* who in order to give her mother nourishment, has had to deprive her child of his rightful due.[299] "They praise excellencies," Reynolds continues, "that can hardly exist together; and above all things, are fond of describing, with great exactness, the expression of a mixed passion, which more particularly appears to be out of the reach of our art."[300] When Reynolds objects to the critics who read mixed passions into painting—and by a mixed passion he means what we have just remarked in Le Brun, the expression of several emotions in a given figure at the same time—or when he later suggests that the painter himself "may have attempted this expression of passions above the powers of his art,"[301] he strikes with the axe of sound common sense at the root of that mistaken tendency of the Aristotelian critics to obscure the legitimate humanistic relationship of the sister arts by declaring in effect that painting, like poetry, is an art of successive events in time. It is both shocking and amusing to contemplate the faults committed by the critics of painting in the name of Aristotle, wherein, it may be observed, the English critics especially outdid themselves. Even if one admits that the original creation and understanding of the figure arts have seldom been the particular forte of the English nation, and if one makes all due allowance for the dominance of *ut pictura poesis* in the late seventeenth century, it is still not easy to understand how a man of the acute critical sense of John Dryden could, in comparing literature with painting, fall into such absurdities as when he compares the subordinate groups gathered about the central group of figures in a painting to the episodes in an epic poem or to the chorus in a tragedy, or the sketch of a painting to stage scenery, or the warts and moles in a portrait to the flaw in the character of a tragic hero.[302] These analogies can scarcely be said to be illuminating, and they show again the confusion that arises when an enthusiastic but befuddled critic naively attempts a comparison of the sister arts that a little reflection on the possibilities and limitations of their media would have shown to be inconsistent with aesthetic truth.

There are occasional hints in Italian criticism of the sixteenth century of trouble to

---

299. Jouin, *op. cit.*, p. 57.

300. *Discourse* v. For an extreme example from the early eighteenth century of what Reynolds objects to, see Richardson's analysis of a painting by Poussin on an episode from Tasso's *Gerusalemme liberata* (*Essay on the Art of Criticism*, p. 196): "The expression of this picture is excellent throughout. The air of Vafrino is just, he hath a character evidently inferior, but nevertheless he appears brave, and full of care, tenderness, and affection. Argante seems to be a wretch that died in rage and despair, without the least spark of piety. Tancred is good, amiable, noble, and valiant, etc., etc" (for several pages). This painting, called *Tancred and Erminia*, and now in the University of Birmingham, is illustrated in Thomas Bodkin, "A Rediscovered Picture by Nicolas Poussin," *Burlington Magazine*, LXXIV, 1939, 253.

301. *Loc. cit.* He refers to Raphael who "has, therefore, by an indistinct and imperfect marking, left room for every

imagination, with equal probability to find a passion of his own."

302. See his *Parallel between Painting and Poetry*, pp. XVII ff. and XLIV ff. But Dryden has also left a most beautifully succinct statement of the comparison of painting with dramatic poetry. In his epistle in verse to Sir Godfrey Kneller, after observing that the stupid people who want nothing but their portraits painted offer no encouragement to one whose métier is the noble art of historical painting, he continues:

"Else should we see your noble Pencil trace
Our Unities of Action, Time, and Place;
A Whole compos'd of Parts, and those the best,
With ev'ry various Character exprest;
Heroes at large, and at a nearer View;
Less, and at distance, an Ignobler Crew;
While all the Figures in one Action joyn,
As tending to Compleat the main Design."

come,[303] but no such gratuitous and strained analogies between poetry and painting as the northern critics finally produced. Some of these have been cited here by way of defining a serious confusion of thought that developed in the later history of the *paragone*, and to show how this confusion was largely the result of the powerful influence of the *Poetics* which in determining the formal character of French classic drama, easily extended itself through the current habit of comparing the sister arts to the criticism of painting as well. It was, of course, the tendency to think of painting in temporal terms, along with the tendency which he was better equipped to oppose, to think of poetry in pictorial terms, that was to provoke the corrective criticism of Lessing in his brilliant attempt to define the limits of poetry and painting.

We are now in a position to see how Lessing's narrow and unsatisfactory conception of bodily beauty as the highest end of painting, which we discussed in an earlier chapter,[304] not only reflects his Neo-Classic taste but also adapts itself readily to his theory of the limits of the arts. For a painting in which clearly-defined physical beauty provides the chief content—in which expression is given but a subordinate place—is unlikely to set the spectator or the critics to dreaming in a literary manner of the thoughts and feelings of the figures as if they were characters in a novel or drama. It is far less likely to do this than an historical painting with its variety of gesture and facial expression, to which Lessing objected precisely because it failed to subordinate expression to bodily beauty. "Beautiful shapes in graceful attitudes," then, since they provide immediate aesthetic satisfaction to the mind which apprehends them in spatial, not temporal terms, are not likely to tempt the imaginative onlooker to undue temporal speculation.

It should not be forgotten, however, that Lessing himself made an important concession to the temporal imagination in his doctrine of the most fruitful moment, according to which the painter who confines himself to a single moment of time must choose that moment in action or emotion—always a moment of relative restraint in which expression will not quarrel with beauty—that will be most suggestive of what is past and of what is still to come.[305] Unfortunately Lessing does not seem to have realized the implications of this doctrine for anything but ancient art. Had he possessed the knowledge or the inclination to apply it fairly to modern art, he might have taken a more charitable view than he did of the element of expression in historical painting. Nevertheless one will note his willingness to consider art not merely as an objective realization of beautiful forms, but in its effect on the imagination, and no critic will seriously disagree with the doctrine of the most fruitful moment, provided it is understood that those images of the past or future which are evoked in the mind are always implicit in the work of art itself, and that they do not expand into actual speculation on the inner life of the figures, or on the temporal stages of the action, that soon leaves the work of art far behind. And Lessing would have been the first to challenge all those for whom the fruitful moment had been entirely too fruitful.

303. Dolce (*Dialogo della pittura*, p. 158), says that the painter must "vada di parte in parte rassembrando il successo della historia" so that the observer will believe that "quel fatto non debba essere avenuto altrimenti di quello, che da lui è dipinto." Thus the painter will never place in front what ought to be behind, etc. It is then remarked that Aristotle in his *Poetics* gave the same advice to dramatists. Notions of time and space as they concern the arts were evidently not altogether clear in Dolce's mind.

304. See pp. 20 ff.

305. *Laokoön* III, and XVI. For the interesting anticipation of Lessing's doctrine in Lord Shaftesbury's discussion of how the painter should represent *Hercules at the Cross-roads*, see Blümner's introduction to his edition of the *Laokoön*, pp. 24 ff.; cf. Howard's edition, pp. LXXV ff.

X— CONCLUSION

In Italy of the sixteenth century the humanistic theory of painting rested on the classical doctrine that "the proper study of mankind is man." All critics assumed that painting, like poetry, was the imitation of human action, and it followed, as this essay has attempted to demonstrate, that it must resemble the sister art in subject matter, in human content, and in purpose. If the painter's inventions were to be comparable to those of the poet in power, depth, or beauty, he must choose themes from ancient and modern poetry, and from history sacred and profane; his genius was said to have its most intimate affinities with the poet's in his power to express human emotion; his aim like the poet's was assumed to be serious, for he must aspire not merely to give pleasure, but to impart wisdom to mankind.[306] This profound relationship with poetry was enough to give to painting the prestige of a liberal art. But to make doubly sure that the painter should never again be considered only an artisan "sans littérature, sans mœurs, sans politesse," the critics, leaning heavily on the example of Pliny who had proclaimed the honorable estate of painters in antiquity, dwelt with wearisome though perhaps pardonable iteration on the free association of painters with princes and learned men during the Renaissance. Lastly, and most important, the high argument of inspired poetry could bestow on painting, as Varchi said in relating Michelangelo's debt to Dante,[307] a profundity of content, a majesty and grandeur that Sir Joshua Reynolds writing of Michelangelo in a later age would have called the sublime.[308] The critics who fashioned the doctrine *ut pictura poesis* thus ranked painting with poetry as a serious interpreter of human life, and the humanistic critic who is deeply concerned with art as a repository of enduring human values will always believe that human life is as supremely the painter's province as it is the poet's, and that some subjects are of more universal interest and importance than others, even though he may not care to admit with Roger de Piles that elevated subject matter can be an actual substitute for original genius.[309]

This was, in fact, De Piles at his most conservative, for although he was never a revolutionary and acquiesced in many of the dictates of the French Academy, his painter's instinct led him to extend a welcoming hand to landscape and still-life, which the Academy held in low repute, just as it led him to object to the unnaturalness of Le Brun's definitions of the passions, and to champion the sensuous element of color without which he said, "contour cannot represent any object as we see it in nature"[310]—a sentiment that was distasteful to the Cartesian academicians who defended contour as the guardian of general, not particular truth. For the rational traditionalism of the Academy, founded on the ideal antique and sustained by a set of thoroughly formalistic concepts, tended to deny the painter his birthright of free converse with a living and unmethodized nature; and although one may discern behind the imposing but uninspired façade of its precepts the belief that the arts should minister to the dignity of human life, the extreme formalism of the academic point of view under Le Brun shows clearly that the once vital humanism of the Renaissance had hardened into inert convention which could not long resist the pressure of new and living forms of expression. And although the doctrine *ut pictura poesis* was to maintain some-

---

306. I must mention here the interesting appearance of the *paragone* in the first scene of Shakespeare's *Timon of Athens*. See A. Blunt, "An Echo of the 'Paragone' in Shakespeare," *Journal of the Warburg Institute*, III, 1938–39, 260–62.

307. *Due lezzioni*, p. 116.

308. *Discourse* xv.

309. *Cours de peinture*, p. 63.

310. *Dialogue sur le coloris*, Paris, 1699, p. 22. In this connection one should point out that the kind of truth which De Piles urged the painter to follow was neither the "Vrai Ideal" of the antique, nor the "Vrai Simple" or natural truth of the Venetians, but what he calls the "Vrai Composé" or "Vrai Parfait"—a combination of the ideal and the natural that only Raphael, he thinks, possessed. This was, of course, to concede far more to nature than Félibien and Le Brun had done. See *Cours de peinture*, pp. 29 ff.

thing better than a hazardous existence during the eighteenth century, it was steadily undermined by forces that were in the long run to make for its destruction. Opposed to the humanistic point of view was the growing interest in external nature, with whose freshness and irresponsible freedom Rousseau, the apostle of emotion, was to contrast the life of human beings freighted with custom and constrained by the "false secondary power" of the reason. And although an interest like De Piles' in the concrete reality of nature as well as in the beauty of her transient effects—in those *formae Veneres fugaces* that had not been lost on Du Fresnoy—was necessary to save the painter's art (as in the Rococo painting of the early eighteenth century it was already doing) from the limitations of academic formalism, it was also a part of that general movement in thought and art away from concentration on the supreme significance of the human image.

Another source of danger to the humanistic point of view during the eighteenth century was the growing importance of the doctrine of original genius which was encouraged by the pervasive influence of the treatise of *Longinus on the Sublime*.[311] And although the Longinian doctrine that the artist, if he is to attain sublimity or greatness, must at times jump the traces of the rules—in Pope's famous phrase "snatch a grace beyond the reach of art"—was accepted by conservative theorists as legitimatizing the occasional flights of genius for which no rules could provide a pattern, as the century progressed it came to be associated in the minds of critics with the subjective and emotional in artistic expression, and with a special class of sublime subjects that were obviously congenial to the romantic temperament and to that alone. And these were non-traditional subjects: scenes for instance of terror, or of vast, wild, and formless nature which had submitted to the laws of order no more than genius itself, it was at length acknowledged, was expected to do. Such a point of view was not one to encourage the ideal representation of human action that had been the theme of humanistic painting, and the doctrine of original genius is, moreover, the ancestor of modern expressionism which is necessarily hostile to the doctrine *ut pictura poesis*. For if the latter is to have any final significance, it must, without denying certain expressive privileges to genius, rest on the principle that since painting like poetry should be most concerned with the interpretation of universal human experience, the painter like the poet must in the act of creation retain a certain power of judgment and selective discrimination that is not compatible with unlicensed self-expression.

Amid the emancipating influences of the eighteenth century Lessing stands out as the last and one of the greatest of the Aristotelians, and the *Laokoön* as one of the last outposts of the humanism of the Renaissance. For in restricting painting and poetry to those subjects that were, as he thought, best suited to their means of imitation, he imposed severely humanistic limitations on both, denying to poetry whose proper sphere he considered to be human action, the description of scenes and objects in nature, and to painting (here, as we have seen, his point of view was narrow and, in a sense, anachronistic) virtually all but the depiction of corporeal beauty. Less brilliant as a dialectician, less uncompromising in his classicism, but, since he was a painter, aware as Lessing could never be of the wide and varied scope of pictorial art, Reynolds was also a late and important exponent of hu-

---

311. This treatise became an important document for European criticism after its translation by Boileau in 1674. Its influence appears already in De Piles' *Abrégé de la vie des peintres* of 1699. For the development of the concept of the sublime in the eighteenth century see S. H. Monk, *The Sublime, a Study of Critical Theories in XVIII-Century England*, New York, 1935. Chap. IX deals with the theories of the sublime among the English critics of painting, and shows how these theories found illustration in the last decades of the century in the painting of the Royal Academy. English art was earlier affected by the sublime than was French art, which did not produce many sublime subjects until the early nineteenth century.

manistic doctrine. And again unlike Lessing he owed much to the doctrine of Longinus, no in its distorted and romantic form, but in its purity—in that form, in fact, in which it had first been known to the late seventeenth century through the translation and commentaries of Boileau. And it is scarcely an exaggeration to say that the emphasis of Longinus on greatness of content in art as opposed to formal beauty, on the artist's power to move the mind through the emotions as against his appeal to the reason, on the imagination which in the greatest art outstrides correct judgment and purity of taste, all served to clear Reynolds' exposition of the academic tradition in his *Discourses* of much of the dead weight of formalism. Moreover it is "that nobleness of conception which goes beyond anything in the mere exhibition of perfect form" and which the painter acquires "by warming his imagination with the best productions of ancient and modern poetry" that is to Reynolds the crown of "that one great idea which gives to painting its true dignity, which entitles it to the name of a liberal art and ranks it as a sister of poetry."[312] Thus one of the last and sanest exponents of the doctrine *ut pictura poesis*—of that doctrine which the Renaissance critics both of painting and poetry based upon the literary theory of antiquity—found that the chief likeness of painting to poetry lay not in adherence to a set of precepts borrowed from the sister art, or in any imagined correspondences of form, but in "nobleness of conception." To Reynolds, the most significant aspect of painting, as of poetry, was its capacity to reveal and interpret the element of dignity in human life. Painting, he believed, is never merely an art of the eye, but it is the mind whose servant the eye is that the painter of genius, like the poet, chiefly desires to address.

APPENDIX I

On the Lack of Ancient Criticism of Painting (*See note 20*)

De Piles says in effect that in ancient times rules were given for painting and poetry, but that both arts after the fall of Rome fell into neglect until later times when Raphael and Titian, Corneille and Racine, tried to restore them to their original perfection. There is, however, this difference between them, that in the case of poetry the works of ancient poets and the rules of Aristotle and Horace are preserved, so that the true idea of poetry has remained as a guide for later poets; whereas in the case of painting, the great works of ancient painters and many critical writings of the Greeks are forever lost, so that, with nothing left to give a just idea of painting as practiced by the ancients in its period of greatest perfection, painting in modern times has not yet been recovered in its fullest extent. But these deficiencies are, he believes, in good part supplied by the works of the best painters who have revived the art, and "by what we gather from those who have laid down the rules of Poesy, as Aristotle and Horace," whereupon he quotes passages from the *Ars poetica* (see notes 14, 15) and the *Poetics* (IV) that indicate a favorable opinion of painting in antiquity. De Piles was thus glad to cite remarks of ancient critics that sustained him in his praise of painting (he remembers with disapprobation another opinion of Aristotle that the arts which require manual performance are

less noble on that account), but, as a progressive critic who admired color and the painting of Rubens, he was unwilling to pay any lip-service to the remains of ancient painting that had come to light in Rome; for in the course of his remarks on the disappearance of the ancient masterpieces of painting, he says bluntly that he holds the Roman remains of little account. No Poussinist would have said so much, no matter how inconsequential the painting. At the end of the sixteenth century Armenini had held a like opinion of the remains of ancient painting. After declaring that his book with its compendium of directions for painters may save them the difficulty and discouragement of long research on their own account, and may even implant in the minds of men a sense of the value of old masterpieces and new that for want of an appreciation of their great worth are falling into decay (rich men in his degenerate age may, he opines, learn from his treatise to become better patrons of the arts), he remarks that painting has suffered for lack of a Vitruvius, and all the more because of its material fragility needs the prescribed word, "perciocchè col mezzo delle scritture, le quali si possono sporgere per tutto il mondo, non solo si rendon facili le arti, e men faticose, ma si conservano ancora più salde, e vive nelle memorie de' posteri, che non si fa quando elle rimangono sola-

312. *Discourse* III.

: nelle lingue di color che le eser-
tuna in questo proposito fu lasciata
ad annichilarsi ed a risolversi in
ie poche pitture ritrovate in luoghi
orrıaı e ınuvnuvn, *da noi dette grottesche, e secondo il*
vocabolo degli antichi, chimere, delle quali, siccome da
piccoli splendori, si tiene che i moderni pigliassero il
modo e la via vera del dipingere. Donde finqui è
manifesto in quanta oscurità di prima si ritrovasse, e
in quanti pericoli gli sia a' di nostri il sentier pre-
cedente" (*De'veri precetti della pittura*, I, I, p. 25).
Armenini was thus no more inclined to worship the
ancient remains of painting than De Piles, and for
less satisfactory reasons.

In the early eighteenth century the scholarly Abbé
du Bos was somewhat more charitably disposed
toward the ancient remains, finding them, so far as
he could tell, equal to the work of the moderns in
design, light and shade, expression, and "composition
poétique," by which he means composition that is
functional to dramatic expression; it is impossible,
he says, to judge their color, but it is evident that
the ancients have not succeeded in "composition
pittoresque" so well as Raphael, Rubens, Veronese,

and others. By "composition pittoresque" Du Bos
means for the most part an harmonious pictorial
effect—good composition for its own sake in the
modern sense of the term. These distinctions are
interesting as pointing to the dissolution of the humanistic point of view and the beginning of modern
aesthetic ideas (cf. note 79). But Du Bos was a
realist and was disinclined to make much of the comparison between ancient and modern painting, so
fragmentary were the ancient remains. And he
takes a fling at modern writers on ancient painting
who, he says, make us more learned, but no more
capable of judging the superiority of ancient to
modern painting (the most famous of such writers
would be Franciscus Junius, the author of *De pictura
veterum*, Amsterdam, 1637). "Ces écrivains," he
adds pointedly, "se sont contentés de ramasser les
passages des auteurs anciens qui parlent de la peinture, et de les commenter en philologues, sans les
expliquer par l'examen de ce que nos peintres font
tous les jours, et mêmes sans appliquer ces passages
aux morceaux de la peinture antique qui subsistent
encore." See his *Réflexions critiques*, I, 38, pp. 370–
409.

APPENDIX 2 (*See note 70*)

INVENTIO, DISPOSITIO, ELOCUTIO

Dolce (*Dialogo della pittura*, p. 174) remarks that
"La inventione vien da due parti, dalla historia e
dall'ingegno del Pittore [the latter becomes, of
course, the all-important part as one approaches the
Romantic Movement at the end of the eighteenth
century; cf. also note 75]. Dalla historia egli ha
semplicemente la materia. E dall'ingegno oltre
all'ordine e la convenevolezza [orderly arrangement
or disposition of figures, and decorum], procedono
l'attitudini, la varietà, e la (per così dire) energia
delle figure, ma questa è parte commune col disegno."
Invention, then, for Dolce, means the choice of the
history that he would represent, and the general
plan of the picture, according to principles of good
disposition and decorum, that he would work out in
his mind. The actual sketch of the picture in black
and white with "the attitudes, variety and energy"
of the figures (all of which would have been perforce
included in a general way, at least, in the invention)
is included under "disegno." Dolce had already
(p. 150) divided the labor of the painter into three
categories: *inventione, disegno,* and *colorito.* "L'inventione," he says, "è la favola, o historia, che'l Pittore
si elegge da lui stesso, o gli è posta innanzi da altri
per materia di quello che ha da operare [this narrow
definition receives subsequently in the dialogue a
broad interpretation of the kind suggested above].
Il disegno è la forma, con che egli la rappresenta
[that is to say the projection into a sketch without
color of the invention in the painter's mind]. Il
colorito serve a quelle tinte, con le quali la natura
dipinge (che così si può dire) diversamente le cose
animate et inanimate" [coloring is, then, the final
rendering of the picture].

It is interesting to observe that Dolce is the first

critic to use this threefold division which corresponds
almost exactly to the first three divisions of the art
of rhetoric—*inventio, dispositio,* and *elocutio*—among
the Roman rhetoricians (Professor Samuel H. Monk
of Southwestern College pointed out to me this and
other interesting examples of the influence of the
rhetoricians on Renaissance and Baroque criticism).
For Cicero and Quintilian as for Dolce *inventio*
means the choice of material, though it also includes
for Dolce, as we have seen above, the general plan
of the composition worked out in the painter's mind
before its execution in a sketch; *dispositio* for the
rhetoricians means a preliminary blocking out of the
oratorical discourse, so as to give a clear indication
of the structural outlines of its final form with the
relation of parts to the whole, just as *disegno* for
Dolce means a preliminary sketch of the painter's
invention; and *elocutio* for the rhetoricians means the
final rendering in language, just as *colorito* for Dolce
means the final rendering in color (see Cicero *De
inventione* I. 7, 9 and cf. *De oratore* I. 31, 142; Quintilian *Institutio oratoria* I. Proœm., 22). A century
before Dolce, Alberti, writing not only in a humanistic spirit, but even more as one interested in the
practice of painting at a time when the Quattrocento
painters were making their realistic advances, divides the art into *circonscriptione, compositione,* and
receptione di lumi (*Della pittura*, pp. 99 ff.). This
order indicates the painter's practical procedure: first
the drawing of figures in outline; second the indication of planes within the outline (this is the first and
purely technical aspect of *compositione;* other aspects
will be mentioned shortly); third, the rendering in
color wherein the painter must be aware of the relation of color to light. Dolce, on the other hand, writ-

ing not as one interested in the technical procedure of the practicing artist, but as an urbane and genial critic with a good education in classical literature and theory in an age that was critical rather than creative, follows the ancient rhetoricians in placing first *inventio*, which includes all of the *preparatory* labor of the painter before he actually begins to work at his canvas: his reading from which he would choose his subject, his conversations with learned men that might provide ideas, and his plan before its actual execution in a sketch for the disposition of his figures in his composition according to the principles of arrangement (*ordine*) and decorum (*convenevolezza*). Alberti's *compositione* corresponds in part to Dolce's *inventione*, for it includes besides the indication of planes in light and shade that distinguishes it in a purely technical sense from *circonscriptione*, the planning of the composition and matters of decorum and expression. Alberti added as a conclusion to his treatise, after *circonscriptione* and *compositione* had been discussed, a short third part that was intended to round out the painter's knowledge and render him "tale che possa seguire intera loda" (*op. cit.*, pp. 143 ff.). It includes a passage containing a few words of advice to the painters to acquire literary and historical knowledge that will improve their ability to compose histories "di cui ogni laude consiste in *la inventione*." This use of the word *inventione* corresponds to its use in Dolce's definition, and it is worth noting that whereas in the realistic Quattrocento literary knowledge is thought of as coming after and crowning the painter's scientific and practical knowledge, in the theoretical Cinquecento it is emphasized as the indispensable propa-

deutic to good painting, being considered equally with genius as the source of invention.

Professor Panofsky has called to my attention the fact that Alberti's threefold division of painting represents an indirect adaptation, long before Dolce's direct adaption, of the rhetoricians' *inventio*, *dispositio*, and *elocutio*: *inventio* being partly included by Alberti under *compositione* (where he speaks of arrangement, decorum, etc.) and mentioned once, in its own name, at the end of his book in connection with his advice concerning literary knowledge; *dispositio*, the preliminary outline of the orator's discourse, being represented also by *compositione* which includes the indication of how "le parti delle cose vedute si porgono insieme in pictura" (p. 109), but also by *circonscriptione*, the outline drawing through which the disposition of figures in a sketch would chiefly be made; and *elocutio*, the actual performance of the oration, by *receptione di lumi*, the rendering of the picture.

It should be noted that Dolce could have found the threefold division of *inventione*, *dispositio*, and *elocutio*, not only in the Roman rhetoricians, but also in Renaissance criticism of poetry which was profoundly influenced by them. See, for instance, Daniello, *La poetica*, Venice, 1536, p. 26: "Dico, tre esser le cose principali dalle quali esso [a poem] suo stato, et suo esser prende. L'Inventione prima delle cose, o vogliam dire, ritrovamento. La Dispositione poi, over ordine di esse. Et finalmente la forma dello scrivere ornatamente le già ritrovate et disposte, che (latinamente parlando) Elocutione si chiama; et che noi volgare, leggiardo et ornato parlare chiameremo."

APPENDIX 3 (*See note 90*)

LOMAZZO ON EXPRESSION

See especially the important passage in *Trattato*, II, 2, pp. 108–109: "In questo loco ragione è che si tratti subsequentemente d'esso moto, cioè con qual arte il pittore habbia da dar il moto alla figura convenientemente; cioè secondo la natura della proportione della forma, e della materia; perche come ho detto, *in questo appunto consiste lo spirito, e la vita dell'arte*; onde i pittori lo sogliono dimandare hora furia, hora gratia, e hora eccellenza dell'arte; e non senza ragione; poiche *questa parte è la più difficile a conseguire che sia in tutta l'arte; et anco la più importante, e più necessaria da sapersi*. Percioche con questa i pittori fanno conoscere differenti i morti da i vivi; i fieri da gl'humili, i pazzi da i savii, i mesti da gli allegri, et in somma tutte le passioni, e gesti che puo mostrare, e fare un corpo humano trà se distinti, che si dimandano con questo nome di moto, non per altro che per una certa espressione, e dimostratione estrinseca nel corpo di quelle cose che patisce internamente l'animo. Che non meno per questa via si conoscono i moti interni delle genti che per le parole anzi più, per operarsi questo dal proprio corpo, ilquale ne più ne meno opera di quello che gli viene ordinato dall'anima rationale rivolta

ò da bene, ò da male secondo l'apprensioni. Et quindi è che i pittori che queste cose intendono benche rari, fanno che nelle sue pitture si veggono quelle maravigliose opere della natura secrete, mosse da quella Virtù motiva che di continuo stando nel cuore nascosta, si dimostra esteriormente nel corpo, e manda fuori i suoi ramoscelli per li membri esteriori, che perciò, secondo quelli si muovono. Quindi nascono quelle meraviglie grandissime de gl'effetti, e dimostrationi delle figure che cosi frà di loro si veggono diversi, come sono differenti le passioni de oro animi; delle quali in questo libro alquanto ne sarà trattato. Ora la cognitione di questo moto, è quella come dissi poco sopra, che nell'arte è riputata tanto difficile, e stimata come un dono divino. *Imperoche per questa parte peculiarmente la pittura si paragona alla poesia*. Che si come al Poeta fà di mestiero ch'insieme con l'eccellenza dell'ingegno habbia certo desiderio et una inclinatione di volontà onde sia mosso à poetare, il che chiamavano gl'antichi furor d'Apollo, e delle muse; cosi ancora al Pittore conviene, che con le altre parti che si gli ricercano habbi cognitione, e forza d'esprimere i moti principali quasi come ingenerata seco, et accresciuta con lui sino dalle fascie: altrimenti è difficile anzi impossibile cosa à possedere perfettamente quest' arte. Si come per esperienza si vede. Che sonosi trovati tanti eccellenti Pittori; si come se ne trovano ancora che nel depingere sono stati da tutti tenuti in grandissimo pregio, si come quelli che rappresentavano le figure vaghe di colori; e bene intese per le membra, e legature d'anatomia benissimo proportionate, e con diligenza allumate di buon chiaro, e scuro à. Mà perche con tutta la cura, e patienza usata non hanno mai potuto acquistar felicemente questa facoltà, hanno lasciato le opere loro sottoposte alla censura de' posteri solamente per le attitudini, et i gesti delle figure mal' espresse, per haverle cavate dalle inventioni altrui, cioè, di coloro che soli nacquero con questa gratia." Cf. Dolce (p. 226): "Finalmente ricerca al Pittore un'altra parte: della quale la Pittura, ch'è priva, riman, come si dice, fredda, et è a guisa di corpo morto, che non opera cosa veruna. Questo è, che bisogna, che le figure movano gli animi de 'riguardanti, alcune turbandogli, altre rallegrandogli, altre sospingendogli a pietà, et altre a sdegno, secondo la qualità della historia. Altrimenti reputi il Pittore di non aver fatto nulla: *perchè questo è il condimento di tutte le sue virtù: come aviene parimente al Poeta, all' Historico, ed all'Oratore: che se le cose scritte o recitate mancano di questa forza, mancano elle ancora di spirito e di vita.*" Cf. with this passage from Dolce the following from Daniello, *La poetica*, p. 40: "*Nè basta solamente che il Poema sia grave, sia vago . . . s'egli non havera poi seco la Persuasione, nella quale tutta la virtù et grandezza del Poeta è riposta. Et pertanto devete affaticarvi figliuoli; di dir sempre*

cose, che seco l'abbino: et che dolcemente gli animi di coloro che ascoltano, o leggono intenerischino et muovino. Il che a voler fare, bisogna prima che voi ottimamente intendiate che cosa gli Affetti siano, o vogliam dir piu tosto le Perturbationi dell'animo possentissimi mezzi a destar nell'altrui menti il pianto, il riso, l'ira, et lo sdegno: et simili." Thus Dolce could have found in Daniello's remarks to the poet concerning expression the precise doctrine that some twenty years later he was to give the painter. Daniello's term *persuasione* comes from the *persuadere* of the Roman rhetoricians which is the equivalent of *muovere*. Roger de Piles at a later day still believed in the supreme importance of expression: "Les Expressions font la pierre de touche de l'esprit de Peintre. Il montre par la justesse dont il les distribue, sa pénétration et son discernement" (*L'idée du peintre parfait*, pp. 43–44). Leonardo, nearly a century before Lomazzo, had defended painting against the implied charge of the proponents of poetry that painting does not express the operations of the mind, by insisting that it does precisely this, provided mental activity is of the kind that can be expressed in bodily movement: "Se la poesia s'estende in filosofia morale, e questa [painting] in filosofia naturale; se quella descrive le operationi della mente, che considera quella, se la mente opera nei movimenti" (*Trattato*, 1, 19). For the concept that bodily movement is expressive of psychic life, cf. in antiquity Cicero *De oratore* III. 57, 216: "Omnis enim motus animi suum quendam a natura habet voltum et sonum et gestum"; III. 59, 222: "Est enim actio quasi sermo corporis, quo magis menti congruens esse debet."

APPENDIX 4 (See note *111*)

The Cartesian Theory of the Passions

In the *Traité des passions* (Art. 6) Descartes says that the body of a living man differs from that of a dead man as a watch or other automaton wound up and running according to the principle of its movement differs from a machine when it is broken and the principle of its movement ceases to operate. The struggle, he says (Art. 47), that people imagine between the higher and reasonable, and the lower and appetitive, parts of the soul, is in reality nothing but a disturbance in the pineal gland that occurs when the *esprits animaux* push the gland from one side while the soul through the agency of the will (which, in this case, resists the passion caused by the movement of the *esprits*) pushes it from the other side. In defining the passions of the soul (Art. 27) as "des perceptions, ou des sentiments, ou des émotions de l'âme, qu'on rapporte particulièrement à elle" (as opposed to other "sentiments" like odors, sounds, and colors, that one refers to exterior objects, or like hunger, thirst, and pain that one refers to the body), Descartes declares that they are caused, maintained, and strengthened by the movement of the *esprits*. These he defines as "un certain air ou vent très subtil" (Art. 7) produced in the brain by a

complex action of the circulation (Art. 10). Set in motion by perception or by the imagination the *esprits* move about the body via the nerves, those "petits tuyaux qui viennent tous du cerveau" (Art. 7), causing the passions of admiration, love, hate, desire, joy, and sadness and the bodily movements and facial expressions that accompany them. Throughout the *Traité des passions*, the passions and their external manifestations are treated as physical reflexes, the inevitable and immediate result of changes in the machine of the body; and it is this mechanistic theory of matter, or "extension" as Descartes calls it, applied to the microcosm of the human body that Le Brun took over when he composed his own treatise on the passions. But Descartes, although he believed that "extension" functioned according to its own mechanical laws, and that no action of the reason or will could prevent experience or recurrence of the passions, believed nevertheless that they could be controlled, and that the man of virtuous life whose conscience never reproached him with having failed to do those things that he judged to be the best would have complete protection against the most violent efforts of the passions to disturb the tranquility of his soul (Art. 148). Furthermore Descartes did not, like the Stoics of antiquity, consider the passions as morbid states of the soul. As a Neo-Stoic of the Baroque age, sharing its fervent interest in the investigation of the physical universe, he considered them "toutes bonnes de leur nature" (Art. 211), believing that they needed only to be controlled; and if those men who were most moved by them experienced the greatest bitterness in life, so did they also taste the greatest sweetness. The soul could have its pleasures apart. But those which it shared with the body depended entirely on the passions (Art. 212).

Le Brun who does not, like the philosopher, view the mechanistic theory of the passions in any larger philosophical perspective, sums it up in the following passage wherein, after stating that ordinarily all that causes passion in the soul causes action in the body (by action he means any movement, bodily or facial), he traces this action back to its source in the circulation of the blood which generates the *esprits:*

"L'action n'est autre chose que le mouvement de quelque partie, et le changement ne se fait que par le changement des muscles, les muscles n'ont de mouvement que par l'extrémité des nerfs qui passent au travers, les nerfs n'agissent que par les esprits qui sont contenus par les cavités du cerveau, et le cerveau ne reçoit les esprits que du sang qui passe continuellement par le cœur, qui l'échaufe et le rarefie de telle sorte qu'il produit un certain air subtil qui se porte au cerveau, et qui le remplit" (*Traité des passions* in Jouin, *Charles Le Brun*, p. 372).

For the debt of the Cartesian physiology to medieval science and to Harvey's theory of the circulation of the blood, see E. Gilson, *Études sur le rôle de la pensée médiévale dans la formation du système cartésien*, Paris, 1930, pp. 51–100.

APPENDIX 5 (See note 112)

SYMPOSIUM ON THE PASSION OF WRATH

It may be interesting to compare some remarks on the expression of the passions by theorists of the sixteenth and seventeenth centuries, noting significant changes as we advance in time and as we move from Italy to northern Europe. Leonardo, for instance, at the end of the Quattrocento gives the painters the following directions for representing the passion of wrath (*Trattato*, III, 381): "Alla Figura irata tenere uno per li capegli col capo storto à terra, et con uno de' gionocchi sul costato, et col braccio destro levare il pugno in alto; questo habbia li capegli ellevati, le ciglia basse e strette, et i denti stretti, et i dui stremi dacanto della bocca archati; il collo grosso, et dinanzi, per lo chinarsi al nemico, sia pieno di grinzi." Leonardo thus thinks of a wrathful figure in actively dramatic terms: his knee is on his enemy's chest, his right fist is raised in the air before the blow is struck, his left hand has seized his enemy by the hair; the movements of the body that express the passion of *ira* have no abstract existence but are represented as Leonardo might have observed them in a Florentine brawl or elsewhere, and the same is true of his remarks on facial expression —the eyebrows low and contracted, the teeth clenched, the corners of the mouth drawn back to produce accentuated curved lines on either side. This passage, which may well be a description of one of Leonardo's own drawings, shows how directly he approached nature in his study of the passions. Lomazzo in defining *ira*, a century later (*Trattato*, II, 11, p. 136) shows none of this realistic approach to nature of the Renaissance but speaks either in generalizations at least entirely the direct sense of observation that one finds in Leonardo, or in terms of examples drawn from books: "L'ira," he writes, "che non è altro che grandissima infiammatione d'animo, fà i moti stizzosi, colerici, e violenti; si come appare in quelli, à cui si gonfia la faccia, gl'occhi s'accendono, et avampano, come bragia; et

i moti di tutte le membra, per l'impeto, e violenza della colera, si fanno gagliardissimi, e molto più risentiti, come in Mosè, quando per l'adoratione dei vitello, ruppe impetuosamente le tavole della legge . . . in Alessandro quando uccise Calistene, e molti suoi amici. Si che ciascuno in quel furore gli sgombrava dinanzi, poiche tanto poteva in lui, che si legge una volta essersi gli veduto in India uscire, e lampeggiar faville di foco dal corpo" (other examples follow). To say as Lomazzo does that the movements of an angry man are "passionate, choleric and violent such as appear in one whose face swells and whose eyes catch fire and burn like coals, whose limbs . . . move most vigorously and in a much more lively fashion (than usual)" is to describe the passion of wrath in very general terms indeed, and one easily detects here, and in Lomazzo's method of piling up examples from books, that same tendency to avoid direct experience of nature that appears in the Mannerist doctrine that the Idea of beauty which the artist should follow is not gathered from nature but exists a priori in his mind, a theory that has its counterpart in the well-known deviations from nature in Mannerist art (see notes 48 and 108). Le Brun, a century after Lomazzo, is not abstract like the latter through imprecision, but because his effort to "préciser les passions" has been carried to such a ridiculous extreme of categorical detail. It is characteristic of Le Brun as a theorist of the north of Europe, with a long artistic tradition behind him of emphasizing the face rather than the body as the chief vehicle of human expression, that he should declare (*Traité des passions* in Jouin, *Charles Le Brun*, p. 377) that "le visage est la partie du corps où elle fait voir plus particulièrement ce qu'elle ressent," and then devote the major part of his treatise to illustrating the changes that occur in the physiognomy under the influence of the passions. Leonardo, as a student of human psychology, was deeply interested in facial expression, but as a southern European with an artistic tradition behind him in which the body is more expressive of human emotion than the face, naturally he was enormously concerned both as an artist and theorist with bodily movement, to which Le Brun in his treatise gives scant attention. Lomazzo is likewise a typical Italian theorist in being far more interested in bodily movement than in facial expression. In the following passage describing chiefly the facial manifestations of the passion of anger, Le Brun like Lomazzo notes the inflamed eyes and swollen face, and he undoubtedly owed to Leonardo, whose *Trattato* was first published in Paris in 1651 with illustrations by Poussin, the bristling hair, swollen neck (neither, be it noted, facial expressions), clenched teeth, and perhaps a hint for what he says about the movement of the eyebrows; for the rest he notes changes of his own prescribing in the pupil, forehead, nostrils, lips, complexion etc., and at the end makes brief reference to one aspect of the internal, physiological cause of the external expression (*ibid.*, p. 387):

"Lorsque la colère s'empare de l'âme, celui qui ressent cette passion, a les yeux rouges et enflâmés, la prunelle égarée et étincelante, les sourcils tantôt abattus, tantôt élevés l'un comme l'autre, le front paroîtra ridé fortement, des plis entre les yeux, les narines paroîtront ouvertes et élargies, les lèvres se pressent l'une contre l'autre, et la lèvre de dessous surmontera celle de dessus, laissant les coins de la bouche un peu ouverts, formant un ris cruel et dédaigneux.

"Il semblera grincer les dents, il paroîtra de la salive à la bouche, son visage sera pâle en quelque endroit, et enflamé en d'autres et tout enflé; les veines du front, des tempes, et du col seront enflées et tendues, les cheveux hérissés, et celui qui ressent cette passion, s'enfle au lieu de respirer, parce que le cœur est oppressé par l'abondance du sang qui vient à son secours."

APPENDIX 6

DECORUM AND VERISIMILITUDE

In Dolce, learning is for the sake of "convenevolezza." In Lomazzo (*Idea*, p. 36) the painter is urged to study continually in the history of all times and of all nations, because history tells us how things happened "in tutti i modi, e con tutte le circonstanze, le quali quanto più minutamente dal pittore sono osservate, et intese, e nell'opere di lui espresse, tanto più fanno la pittura *simile ad vero*." But this truth to fact is for the sake of a becoming majesty and grandeur "che doveva essere nel proprio fatto." In Félibien, as we have seen, learning is chiefly for the sake of "bienséance" (see p. 41) or decorum, although "vraisemblance" or verisimilitude which Félibien interprets in the sense of the Aristotelian τὸ εἰκός—probability—would also result from the painter's learning. This might have been the case, for instance, in Veronese's *Supper at Emmaus* in which, however, the disposition of the place and all the people about our Lord "ne conviennent point à cette action" (Preface to the *Conférences*, pp. 314-15). But this last phrase and the example chosen show how closely Aristotle's concept of the probable, which is central to his doctrine of typical imitation, tended in Félibien's mind to merge with the concept of the appropriate and becoming.

Some fifty years later (1719) Du Bos, whose native realism that was often damaging to the doctrines of the Academy probably led him to resent the conventionalizing implications of the term decorum, talks only of "vraisemblance," which he divides into two parts: "vraisemblance mécanique" and "vraisemblance poétique" (*Réflexions critiques*, I, 30, pp. 268 ff.). The former consists, he says, "à ne rien représenter qui ne soit possible, suivant les loix de la statique, les loix du mouvement, et les loix de l'optique." This adherence to the truth of natural law, a reaffirmation of northern realism after two centuries of Mannerist and classical art in France,

not to mention the formalistic theory of the Academy, coincides, interestingly enough, with the realistic reaction against classicism in the contemporary style of the Rococo. But "vraisemblance poétique" on close examination turns out to be little more than the Horatian and Renaissance decorum, cleansed, however, of all implications of the instructive or edifying; for Du Bos admitted that art should give pleasure but denied that it should also instruct (see note 135). It is clearly more closely related to Horatian and Renaissance decorum than to Aristotelian probability, although Du Bos certainly had the latter in mind as well. And if Dolce's "convenevolezza" were substituted in the following passage (*ibid.*, p. 269) for "vraisemblance poétique," a phrase which Du Bos owed to his interest in the drama and in dramatic theory, there would be absolutely no difference in the sense: "La vraisemblance poétique consiste à donner à ses personnages les passions qui leur conviennent, suivant leur âge, leur dignité, suivant le tempérament qu'on leur prête, et l'intérêt qu'on leur fait prendre dans l'action. Elle consiste à observer dans son tableau ce que les Italiens appellent *il Costumé*, c'est-à-dire, à s'y conformer à ce que nous sçavons des mœurs, des habits, des bâtimens et des armes particulières des peuples qu'on veut représenter. La vraisemblance poétique consiste enfin à donner aux personnages d'un tableau leur tête et leur caractère connu, quand ils en ont un, soit que ce caractère ait été pris sur des portraits, soit qu'il ait été imaginé."

Two years after Du Bos' book appeared, Antoine Coypel published his *Epître à mon fils*, a short compendium in verse of what he considered it essential for the painter to know; that is a kind of pendant to Boileau's *L'art poétique*; and it was, in fact, Boileau who urged him to publish his verse epistle and the *Dissertations* that are a commentary upon it (see

Jouin, *op. cit.*, pp. 367 ff.). In the latter, after listing a formidable array of subjects in which the painter must be learned, Coypel distinguishes (*ibid.*, p. 333) between characters taken from history which must be "semblables" and those from fable which must be "convenables." Here "semblable" which equals "vraisemblable" (Coypel uses both terms interchangeably) has not the sense of the probable which it had for the classicizing theorists of the seventeenth century, who were close to the Aristotelian theory of poetry as illustrated in the French classical drama, and which it had partially in the mind of Du Bos. It means rather "like the truth" in the sense of adherence to fact, a meaning which it had also, at times, in Italian literary criticism of the sixteenth century, in Castelvetro, for instance, where this meaning coexists with the Aristotelian meaning of the probable (See Charlton, *Castelvetro's Theory of Poetry*, pp. 41 ff.). If he is painting history, then, the painter is learned for the sake of "vraisemblance" in the sense that he will get his facts straight, but, Coypel does not add, as Félibien would have added, for decorum's sake, and it is interesting that he is far enough removed from the tradition of Félibien and Le Brun to hold of little account those rules for decorum that would maintain the dignity of religious subjects by imposing restraint on the rendering of "basses circonstances" like the ox and the ass in the Nativity. The latter, Coypel agrees, should not be played up, "but whatever rules one may establish in this regard are always unfruitful if they are not sustained by the painter's judgment and delicacy of spirit" (*ibid.*, p. 282). But decorum or the "convenable" is for Coypel merely the proper form for rendering the figures of fable according to their recognized characters, and to illustrate this rather narrow meaning of the term, which appears in Horace as a kind of corollary to the larger meaning of decorum as that which is appropriate to the typical rendering of human life, he quotes the famous lines of the Roman poet about preserving the traditional characters of Achilles, Medea, Ixion, etc. (*Ars poetica* 119–27). But the painter may, however, says Coypel, in the case of historical pictures, leave the "vraisemblance" to follow the "convenable" and, without losing sight of his characters, embellish their portraits. Here "convenable" seems to mean to idealize in a manner appropriate to the historical characters whom the painter will treat. But the upshot of the whole matter in Coypel is that the notions of "vraisemblance" and decorum which had definite meaning in the minds of the Academicians of the time of Le Brun have here largely lost their original force, and are treated in a way that marks, even in a man who in many ways is still steeped in doctrines of the Academy, the beginnings of the dissolution of that point of view. For Coypel "vraisemblance" no longer means, as we have seen, the probable, but truth to historical fact; decorum has only the limited meaning of the traditionally appropriate rendering of characters from fable, or occasionally of personages from history, and its connotations of the decent and becoming in the moral or religious sphere that were strong in Félibien and Le Brun, have for Coypel no more than for Du Bos any significance in the domain of the rules, but are subject to the artist's personal taste. The notion of decorum is still inconsistently present in 1765 in Diderot for all his insistence that "nature never makes anything incorrect" ("Essai sur la peinture" in *Œuvres complètes*, ed. Assezat, Paris 1876, p. 461 and p. 487). But in his fourth *Discours*, delivered in 1771, Reynolds practically limits his remarks on decorum to the following: "Those expressions alone should be given to the figures which their respective situations generally produce. Nor is this enough; each person should also have that expression which men of his rank generally exhibit. The joy, or the grief, of a character of dignity is not to be expressed in the same manner as a similar passion in a vulgar face." In these remarks the elaborate rules of the French Academy have given way to a mere hint. As for verisimilitude, its meaning of factual truth does not exist in Reynolds who knew, furthermore, that "particularities" are inconsistent with the grand style; and its Aristotelian meaning of probability is not mentioned but is subsumed in Reynolds' discussion of typical representation. Thus in the course of the eighteenth century, those concepts that had been of great importance in the doctrine *ut pictura poesis* during its heyday under Le Brun come to be seen in proper perspective or to disappear. The antiformalistic tendencies that were to culminate in the Romantic Revival, and to which Reynolds was sensitive, were enough virtually to dispose of decorum to which the Aristotelian "vraisemblance" had in the seventeenth century, as we have seen, been closely related.

INDEX

ILLUSTRATIONS

Fig. 1   Paris, Louvre: Poussin, *Fall of the Manna in the Wilderness*

Fig. 2   Moscow, Pushkin Museum: Poussin, *Armida and the Sleeping Rinaldo*

Fig. 3 Chantilly, Musée Condé: Poussin, Drawing after an Antique
Sarcophagus, *Selene and Endymion*

Fig. 4 Paris, Louvre: Drawing of an Antique Sarcophagus with Putti,
Last Homecoming of Meleager (from Robert)

Fig. 5   Windsor Castle, Royal Library: Drawing after an Antique
Sarcophagus, *Selene and Endymion*

Fig. 6 Rome, Cloister of San Paolo fuori-le-mura: Drawing of an
Antique Sarcophagus, *Selene and Endymion* (from Robert)

Fig. 7   Detroit, Institute of Arts: Poussin, *Selene and Endymion*

Fig. 8 Paris, Guyot de Villeneuve Collection: Vouet, *The Abduction of Rinaldo*

Fig. 9   Rome, Borghese Gallery: Raphael, *Entombment*

Fig. 10   Stockholm, National Museum: Pietro da Cortona (?),
Abduction of Rinaldo

Fig. 11   Poussin, *Abduction of Rinaldo* (Engraving by Massé)

Fig. 12 Windsor Castle, Royal Library: Michelangelo, *Children's Bacchanal* (Drawing)

Fig. 13   Marcantonio Raimondi, *Judgment of Paris*: Engraving after
Drawing by Raphael

Fig. 14   Rome, Palazzo Costaguti: Guercino, *Rinaldo in Armida's Chariot*

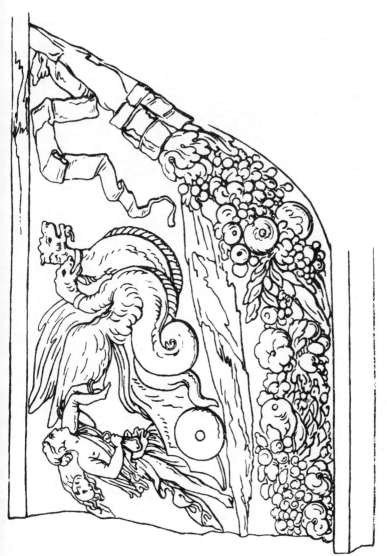

Fig. 15 Drawing of a Lost Fragment of an Antique Sarcophagus, *Flight of Medea* (from Robert)

Fig. 16 *Flight of Medea:* Woodcut Illustration for Ovid's
Metamorphoses, Lyons, 1559

Fig. 17 Paris, Guyot de Villeneuve Collection: Vouet, *Warriors in Armida's Garden*

Fig. 18 Brussels, Royal Museum: Annibale Carracci, *Diana and Actaeon*

Fig. 19   Castello, *Warriors in Armida's Garden:* Illustration
for Tasso's *Gerusalemme Liberata*, 1617

Fig. 20 *Diana and Actaeon*: Engraved Illustration for Ovid's *Metamorphoses*, Paris, 1619

Fig. 21   Pompeii, House of Sallust: *Diana and Actaeon*

Fig. 22 Naples, National Museum: Annibale Carracci, *Rinaldo and Armida*

Fig. 23 *Venus and Adonis:* Woodcut Illustration for Ovid's
Metamorphoses, Lyons, 1559

Fig. 24   Castello, *Rinaldo and Armida:* Illustration for Tasso's
Gerusalemme Liberata, 1590

Fig. 25   Conversano, Castello: Paolo Finoglio, *Rinaldo and Armida*

Fig. 26 Chicago, Art Institute: Tiepolo, *Rinaldo and Armida*

Fig. 27   Conversano, Castello: Paolo Finoglio, *Rinaldo Abandons Armida*

Fig. 28 Paris, Louvre: Poussin, *Rinaldo Abandons Armida* (Drawing)

Fig. 29 Pompeii, House of the Tragic Poet: *Theseus Abandons Ariadne*

Fig. 30 Rome, Vatican: Hadrianic Relief, *Theseus Abandons Ariadne*

Fig. 31 Paris, Guyot de Villeneuve Collection: Vouet, *Rinaldo Abandons Armida*

Fig. 32 Antonio Tempesta: *Rinaldo Abandons Armida* (Engraving)

NORTON LIBRARY TITLES IN
ART, ARCHITECTURE AND THE PHILOSOPHY OF ART